NOT FOR RESALE
DISTRIBUTE THRU
BALTIMORE CITY HEALTH DEPARTMENT

D1088929

Western
Horsemanship
and
Equitation

Western Horsemanship *and* Equitation

Dwight Stewart

ARCO PUBLISHING COMPANY, INC.
NEW YORK

Published by Arco Publishing Company, Inc.
219 Park Avenue South, New York, N.Y. 10003

Copyright © 1979 by Dwight Stewart

Portions of this book were originally published in
Western Equitation, Horsemanship, and Showmanship,
copyright © 1973 by Dwight Stewart.

All rights reserved. No part of this book may be
reproduced, by any means, without permission in
writing from the publisher, except by a reviewer
who wishes to quote brief excerpts in connection
with a review in a magazine or newspaper.

Library of Congress Cataloging in Publication Data

Stewart, Dwight.
  Western horsemanship and equitation.

  Originally published by Vantage Press, New York.
  Bibliography: p. 261
  Includes index.
  1. Western riding. 2. Horse-training.
I. Title.

SF309.3S78   1977   789'.2   76–45386
ISBN 0-668-04044-0 (Library Edition)

Printed in the United States of America

Preface

A writer can mislead a lot of people. To write well he must know his subject thoroughly. Dwight Stewart knows horses and horsemanship as few people do.

For five decades Dwight Stewart has bred, trained, and shown fine horses. At the age of five, his father set him astride an old gray mare, starting a love affair that has lasted into the present.

When Dwight turned sixteen, his family moved to California. Here he learned the unhurried training methods of the Spanish Dons. These methods of schooling the young horse to hackamore, bit, saddle, and leg resulted in a supple, responsive mount much to young Stewart's liking. These methods are integral to the Stewart style of teaching horse and rider.

As a young trainer Dwight Stewart had to take the wilder, more cantankerous horses. He has been kicked, bitten, bucked off, rolled on, dragged, and run away with. Despite all of this, Dwight Stewart has survived and prospered.

Today, twenty-four Quarter Horse Champions and countless horsemen give Dwight Stewart credit for their successes. The great Quarter Horse Stallion Major Thunder—a Champion of Champions—is one of these. First started by Lanham Riley, then finished and owned by Dwight, Major Thunder's record fills four pages of the Quarter Horse Record.

Dwight has established and operated successful training stables in California, Nevada, and Arizona and today operates from his ranch in Texas. He is past president of both the California Cutting Horse Association and the Arizona Professional Horsemen's Association. He holds both AHSA and AQHA judge cards.

Dwight Stewart and his wife Ruth have accompanied me on tour-studies of more than twenty countries. Dwight was my instructor in both the Horse Science School and the Stud Managers' School. During our long acquaintance I have become aware of his tremendous horse "savvy" and love of teaching.

I take pleasure in recommending *Western Horsemanship and Equitation* to all horse lovers. It's an authoritative treatise.

Dr. M. E. Ensminger, Ph.D.
President, Agriservices Foundation
3699 East Sierra Avenue
Clovis, California 93612

Acknowledgments

Acknowledgments and very grateful thanks are due to the following for without their help this book would have never been written:

Linda Anderson
Cedar Hills, Texas

Jack and Linda Baker
Thousand Oaks, California

Ray Bankston (Dalco)
Irving, Texas

Jack Barcus
Las Vegas, Nevada

Harold Campton
Bethel, Ohio

Chris Cason
Hillsboro, Texas

M. L. Davis, Photographer
Las Vegas, Nevada

Carol Dickinson, Photographer
Calahan, Colorado

Kenny Dunlap
Prescott, Arizona

Ki Ki Ebsen
Thousand Oaks, California

M. E. Ensminger, Ph.D.
Clovis, California

Frank Evans
El Cajon, California

June Fallow
Pittsburg, California

C. T. Fuller
Catasaqua, Pennsylvania

Dan Grigorercu
Bucarest, Rumania

Kathy Hale
Dallas, Texas

Barbara Hansen
Thousand Oaks, California

Jane Hastings
Waxahachie, Texas

Carl and Arline Helm
Los Angeles, California

Henry Hite
Milford, Texas

Marilyn Hite
Milford, Texas

Patty and Warren Hveem
Las Vegas, Nevada

Marquellou Ingram
Mesquite, Texas

Johnny Johston
Los Angeles, California

Bob Jones
Fresno, California

Clyde Kennedy
Sun Valley, California

Susan Kieckhefer
Prescott, Arizona

Mike and Millie Leonard
Milford, Texas

Jerry Levi
New Orleans, Louisiana

Vladimir Littauer
Syosset, New York

Mike MacDowell
Las Vegas, Nevada

Tommy Manion
Springfield, Illinois

Joan and Fred McDougal
Shadow Hills, California

Mac and Maggi McHugh
Diamond Bar, California

Victor S. Myers, D.V.M.
University of Minnesota

Scott Nicolaides
Thousand Oaks, California

Vaughn Olsen
San Bernardino, California

Luis Ortega
Paradise, California

Trisha Parker
Dallas, Texas

Parr's Cameras
Dallas, Texas

Drs. Putnam and Ables, D.V.M.
Burleson, Texas

Drs. Edward and Lee Putnam
Yuma, Arizona

Frances Reker
Rockford, Minnesota

Ronnie Richards
Chino, California

Lanham Riley
Aledo, Texas

Matlock Rose
Gainesville, Texas

Lynn Rubel
Prescott, Arizona

Louise Serpa
Tucson, Arizona

Lynn and Harry Stickler
Watsonville, California

J. Leroy Weathers
Phoenix, Arizona

Jimmy Williams
Flint Ridge, California

John A. Wilson, Professor of Geology
University of Texas at Austin

B. F. Yeates, Horse Extension Speciali
Texas A & M University

Contents

Introduction

This book does not pretend to be the last word in equitation, horse-manship, and showmanship. Many changes have taken place in the past and opinions are constantly changing. Trends in riding come and go. I find that I am still learning better ways to school the horse.

After more than fifty years of riding and training horses I believe that it is possible for a horse to be schooled in a kind and humane manner. This can be done by gaining his confidence and friendship, and bringing him slowly through a training course in which each lesson is mastered before the next is started.

I believe I have developed an easy method of teaching riding so that both youngsters and adults can compete successfully in horse shows.

The methods and opinions expressed here are my own. They are those that work for me, but I don't claim that they are the only ones.

I would like this to be a reference book for the times when you don't know what to do. I believe that every problem with a horse has a solution, and I hope you will find the answer in these pages.

Chapter 1

Horse Psychology

Have your horse's actions ever bewildered you? Have you been amazed at how he thinks, astonished at his extraordinary memory? If you have, then join the many others who wonder. Admit to your interest in horse psychology. Although, to many, psychology evokes thoughts of sex or long columns of figures, it is more than that; it is the study of the mind.

Experimentation and study have not explained all the mysteries of the horse's mind. There are still many areas to be considered. As a true horse buff, bitten by the horse bug with no chance of kicking the habit, you have probably tried to find the answers to some of these vexing problems. So, this study of horse psychology may help you understand how your horse thinks and why he acts as he does.

We must accept the fact that training and riding are inseparable. Whether you ride for pleasure, are a rancher or cowboy who rides to tend the stock, a trainer at the racetrack, or a trainer of show horses, training can't be divorced from riding. The act of riding can be spelled equitation and the equestrian must know the principles of training to get his horse to obey him easily. One must ride well to train the horse, for the horse is learning each time he is ridden. Consequently, the trainer needs to know the principles involved or he may teach the horse bad habits.

The horse's feelings must be considered whether you are a trainer or a pleasure rider. If you want a horse that is quiet, supple, obedient, and a pleasure to ride, use neither fear nor force as a basic training method.

We must consider riding healthful, out-of-doors exercise. It is recommended by prominent physicians as it uses nearly every muscle in the body, especially the stomach muscles.

After spending more than five decades breeding, training, and judging horses, I believe that a brief look at the horse's history will help us to understand him better. We know that thousands of years ago he lived in the swamps. At that time, the horse was about the size of a large dog, and his feet were much like those of the modern dog. This horse is called Eohippus (*see* Fig. 1). Through the ages he moved to the plains and hills where his feet changed until the middle toe became the hoof on which he now walks.

On the plains, horses roamed in bands for protection and company, for they are extremely gregarious animals, a characteristic which accounts for their reluctance to leave other horses. Each band had a leader (*see* Fig. 2), usually the senior stallion, who watched over the band and sounded the alarm when danger threatened. The horse's best defense was flight. They are not fighters unless cornered. From this we can understand why they still run away when frightened. Many claim these actions are caused by instinct and this may be so.

As the horse grew in size his brain failed to grow proportionately. The brain is still about the size it was five thousand years ago and compared to the size of his head it is quite small.

The horse, accustomed to a leader, lacked initiative and this is probably one of the reasons why he accepted domestication. The process of domestication was long and complicated, but herd animals are easier to domesticate than solitary ones. The horse likes someone to do his thinking for him. He likes a leader, enjoys routine, organization, and resents change.

Horses are timid, and so courage can only be built up if he believes in his trainer and rider. He needs guidance and soon loses courage if his rider loses his. If the rider fears a jump that the horse is approaching, the horse becomes frightened. Both riders and horses lose their courage and confidence when asked to perform beyond their ability.

Confidence may well be the most important word in dealing with horses. The horse must have confidence in his handler and trainer. He must have faith in them and believe they will neither harm nor abuse him. A great Greek statesman and general, Xenophon, wrote a book entitled *The Art of Horsemanship*, about twenty-four centuries ago. Any horse expert who has studied this book must be impressed by the clarity of the author's statements and his knowledge of the horse's feelings. His training was based on kind treatment, a method which, unfortunately, is not always followed today. Xenophon said: "Anything forced and misunderstood can never be beautiful."

The horse must have another kind of confidence: a belief in his ability to do what is asked of him. This is not a new concept for, to quote Xenophon: "Young horses should be trained in such a way that

Fig. 1. Artist's concept of Eohippus, the early horse.

Fig. 2. A herd of mares shows the horse's preference for others of its kind.

they not only love their riders but look forward to the time they are with them."

Many horsemen, authors, and experts believe that the horse is two-sided; that there is little connection between the two sides of his brain. Therefore, the horse is taught as though he were two horses, with each side schooled individually. They feel that although the horse can learn everything on one side, the other will have to be taught as well.

The horse's brain is not completely bifurcated for it has been proven that the optic nerves cross over. The left optic nerve ends up on the right side of the brain and part of the fibers of the right eye end up on the left side of the brain.

The exact cause and the extent of the horse's two-sidedness is not understood, but every trainer must consider this condition and teach both sides of the horse.

Upon further examination, we find that each horse is different, that some are more two-sided than others. There can be no doubt that any lesson taught on one side will be taught more easily on the other. For example, a horse that has been taught the shoulder-in (sidepass) to the right can be taught the same thing to the left in much less time.

So, we must conclude that there has not been enough study of the horse's mind. All that we really know has been accumulated through the experiences of horsemen and handed down through the years to succeeding generations.

Closely related to this concept of the division of the brain is the fact that horses, like humans, are left or right oriented. To keep the horse even, the trainer must spend more time training one side than the other. Also, one side of the horse's mouth may be more sensitive than the other and so the trainer must use one rein differently from the other to keep the horse traveling straight.

Captain Vladimir S. Littauer, considered by many to be the finest horseman in the United States, asserts: "The distinct unevenness in the horse's sides, which is sometimes encountered, has not given me much trouble in schooling, and this defect was easily corrected in almost all cases."

Captain Littauer is an authority on a distinct method of schooling and riding country-hacks, hunters, and jumpers. This method is called *forward riding*, and is described in his two popular books *Common-sense Horsemanship* (1972) and *Schooling Your Horse* (1956).

Charles Chenevix-French in his *History of Horsemanship* (1970) wrote: "Colonel Chamberlin . . . had an influence on American riding second only to that of Vladimir Littauer, who set up the Boots and Saddles Riding School in New York in the 1920s . . . All that was lacking to American Horsemanship at the beginning of the twentieth century was the educated, scientific horsemanship of France and Italy . . . but this deficiency was made good between 1920 and 1939 by some very gifted horsemasters and equitation instructors, notably Vladimir Littauer, formerly of the Imperial Russian Army, who . . . profoundly influenced civilian riding, and Colonel Chamberlin."

Captain Littauer believes that an uneven mouth is usually the result of the rider's uneven hands. To correct this defect, he recommends that the rider "vibrate" the rein on the stiff side the moment this side leans on the rider's hands. The rider should not pull on this side for this enables the horse to lean more easily.

Many westerners resent terms and training methods that are used in the English style of riding, and not all of these may be adapted to western ways, but many of these methods should be used with both styles. One method that surely fits both styles is riding with a rein in each hand. The horse must be taught to travel straight, not only with his head and neck directly in front of him, but with his hind legs following straight behind the forelegs. Many young horses develop the bad habit of carrying their heads to one side and watching their riders out of one eye. This must not be allowed. Many problems will arise from this as the green horse advances in his training.

Very few horses travel straight of their own accord. It is up to the rider to teach this important lesson. It is much easier to start the young horse correctly than to correct a bad habit after it has been acquired.

Reasoning is the horse's greatest weakness. He has little ability to make judgments, form conclusions, or arrive at a logical explanation for some new or unexpected occurrence. The smartest horse cannot compete with a mule, or equal a chimpanzee, or even a dog.

For instance, a chimpanzee can be taught to imitate humans. Many dogs can be taught to fetch the paper or bring the cows from the pasture, all for a pat on the head. A mule will never overeat, or stampede and run blindly into a fence or an automobile, both things horses often do.

Reasoning and intelligence, as defined by the dictionary, seem to mean about the same thing: the capacity for understanding, grasping truths and facts in a clear logical manner. This is not the approach used by the horse. He will not concentrate on any difficult problem, of his own accord.

We often hear some owner tell of his horse's intelligence, citing instances of his accomplishments, such as how he learned to open the bolt on his stall door. This is more fondness than fact. While this action may involve a great deal of ingenuity on the horse's part he probably learned to do it by accident.

Each horse is an individual. Set up a training course and at its end each horse *should* be able to do all the things taught in the course. However, we sometimes find great differences. Some horses learn very quickly, while others have tempers, are lazy, are nervous, lack ability, or are real athletes.

A dog will do many things because of affection for his owner or trainer, but this is not so with the horse. He will not perform or do tricks for a pat. He loves to be petted, loves sugar or tidbits, but will not perform for them alone. If sugar or tidbits are to be given, do it during the lesson, immediately after the horse has done what was asked of him, for the horse's ability to associate two separate actions is very short—some say no longer than three seconds.

The horse has a keen sense of smell and depends on it to identify food it wants to eat and to discard food to which it objects. For this reason it is very difficult to mix a worm powder in a horse's grain (especially the second time) for many horses will push it aside and refuse to eat it. Taste and smell are hard to separate as the horse will refuse things by smell and eat others with a strong odor and refuse them by taste.

His sense of touch is highly developed and the areas around his extremities are very sensitive. This is readily discernible by trying to touch a young horse around the mouth or trying to pick up his feet.

Contact between man and horse is established by the tactile sensation of the skin. Just under the skin lies the panniculus muscle which covers a great part of the horse's body. This muscle wrinkles the skin when it contracts, as when a horse shivers, or "rattles" his skin after rolling. It is also the muscle he uses to shake flies from his skin where his tail will not reach.

The skin over his ribs is also sensitive. The rider uses this place to contact and control the horse by use of his legs, spurs, or whip. The hands contact the horse's mouth through the reins and bit. Here, man can depend on his hands to convey a message to the horse. The trainer must have good hands and remember that to secure obedience, force is applied only when necessary and only as strongly as that particular incident requires.

Hearing and sight in the horse usually work together. His ears usually point in the direction he is looking, though not always. His hearing, like the dog's, is better than that of humans. He can locate the source of a sound much better than we can.

The horse's vision differs from that of humans. He uses a different method of focusing his eyes on near or distant objects. Most animals (among them man) focus their vision by altering the shape of the lens, or by moving the lens toward or away from the cornea. While the retina in these animals is regularly concave, in the horse it is irregularly concave, nearer the cornea at some spots than at others. This is known as a ramped retina. The horse produces the best visual image, upon the cornea, by raising or lowering his head. If he is ridden with a martingale, a tie-down, or a tight rein he can't raise his head and stretch his neck as a horse likes to do when coming to a jump, and so cannot see very well.

There is little doubt that the horse sees two pictures at the same time, one with either eye, except when both eyes are focused to the front, at which time he can't see anything on either side. However, even when the head and neck are straight ahead the horse has some posterior vision. Watch the horse's ears to know in which direction he is looking. If he is looking back, raise your hand or whip and he will see it immediately.

Horses seem to see farthest when standing still with their heads up and muzzles nearly perpendicular. They seem to see very little of objects at a distance until they move, then, they attract their attention. Unable to concentrate long on anything the animals soon decide to retreat or to disregard the object they were viewing.

Although this book deals primarily with the western horse there are many things that can be better illustrated by referring to the horse trained for the English saddle.

When a horse comes to a jump he gives it his complete attention. As he nears it his neck is outstretched and his head slightly raised, so that both eyes are focused on the obstacle. Many trainers believe that when the horse gets about four feet from the jump he can no longer see it and jumps blind. They feel that this is the cause of many refusals. Whether or not this is true is debatable. Other trainers believe that the horse sees the obstacle when taking off and this determines the character of the jump. These trainers believe that after the take-off the horse doesn't need to see the jump. Captain Littauer remarks that sometimes a poor jumper may look down during the flight and spoil the jump by doing so.

Those who ride a trail horse are aware of the fact that he must lower his head to inspect the obstacle he is approaching, and when he does so

Fig. 3. A horse will lower its head to examine an obstacle. (Chuck Kelly on West-phall Topper.)

Fig. 4. A horse may shy at something completely harmless. (Darrel Nickerson on Snap Bottom Rey.)

he has a much better chance of negotiating it properly. (*See* Fig. 3.)

Most animals are said to be color-blind, and this seems to apply to the horse. He can see shades of gray, dark areas, shadows, and mosaics, but he can't identify green grass from a distance. He can see objects ahead but may mistake them and shy at something completely harmless. (*See* Fig. 4.)

Just how color-blind a horse may be has not yet been completely ascertained. A shy horse who has been used to proceeding over obstacles with blue rails may refuse when they are replaced with red ones. We can only conclude that there has not been enough study of the workings of the horse's brain.

That the horse is unable to concentrate for long periods of time is recognized, so any lesson requiring close attention from the horse must not last longer than ten or fifteen minutes. At the end of this concentrated period the horse should be stopped, preferably in the center of the ring, allowed to relax, petted on the neck, shoulders, and hips, and encouraged by the rider's voice. When he has relaxed, he should be allowed to walk quietly for a few minutes and then the lesson may be resumed. Lessons must not be continued until the horse is exhausted, angry, or bored, or he will begin to develop bad habits such as switching his tail, carrying "sour" ears (ears laid back), and shaking his head.

Any discussion of horse psychology must include reward and punishment. Again we can quote Xenophon: "Punishment must never be administered in anger, because an action committed in anger will later be regretted." Nearly twenty-four hundred years later the directions for the cavalry of the Australian Army read: "Punishment must never be administered in anger." The horse's confidence can be destroyed in just one fight and weeks of work undone in a few minutes.

Before punishing a horse, the rider must be sure that the horse is disobedient and *not* that he misunderstands. If he is sure, then punishment must come immediately; some horsemen say it must come within three seconds in order for the horse to associate the punishment with the infraction.

There are many ways to gain a horse's confidence and make him like his schooling. Rewards will make him grateful and willing to satisfy his trainer. A reward suggested by Xenophon to come at the end of the lesson: "The rider should there and then dismount and lead his horse back to the stable, not ride him back." (*See* Fig. 5.)

Horsemanship, equitation, and horse psychology are so intricately woven together that no horseman can be successful without under-

Fig. 5. Reward your horse: lead him back to the stable after a lesson.

standing and using all three. It has been said that a horse changes from day to day, depending on his disposition, breeding, temperament, his handler, and the weather.

Knowledge of horse psychology can be applied as a help in training. He needs sympathy and understanding of his mentality. Confidence is absolutely essential for he stiffens up when afraid or nervous and then cannot relax. Without relaxation, suppleness cannot be taught. Some trainers have said that for teaching to be effective, it must be understood, and to be understood it must be effective.

Chapter 2
The Longe Line

Time! The problem of every horse trainer and even the pleasure rider who rides an hour in the evening or on a weekend is time. The young horse must be schooled and the pleasure horse exercised or his stall becomes a jail.

The longe line is one of the best time-savers at the trainer's disposal. We don't know who originated it, but there is nothing new about it. History mentions longeing as early as the sixteenth century. It is an excellent way of gaining the confidence of a young horse, of teaching it obedience, quieting it down, and giving it needed exercise.

The colt can be taught to go forward freely, to improve his balance by working in a circle, as well as stretching his muscles, flexing his spine, and bending his neck. If these things are taught to him while he is not carrying weight, it is easier for him to learn, and it avoids injury in the case of a young horse whose bones are not set. It is also a method of exercise for the horse who cannot be ridden, as well as an accepted way of introducing a horse to jumping.

Some trainers use the longe more than others; young trainers are anxious to ride the colt as soon as possible while older trainers are willing to spend more time in preparation. Some of the greatest longe line advocates do not ride at all. There can be no doubt that any time spent teaching obedience and gaining the horse's confidence will be apparent when he is ridden.

Anyone, even a child, can learn to longe a horse and perhaps for this reason we find many western trainers who will not use it. However, the most successful trainers longe their horses and can teach many things from the ground.

Every step in horse training must be carefully planned and have a definite place in the trainer's schedule, for the horse must advance step-by-step in his training toward that time when he is light, supple, and a pleasure to ride. The initial work is done on the ground and the trainer must remember that he is creating a set of habits which will last throughout the life of the horse. The trainer must command obedience yet he wants his horse to appear as free and happy under saddle as he does in the pasture.

There is no way the trainer can improve on the *natural* manner of the horse as he moves with his head up, his neck arched, his ears pricked forward, his tail high, and toes hardly touching the ground. What the trainer must do is teach the horse confidence. Lessons in confidence start when the horse learns to lead. He must be taught to lead freely; he must walk beside the trainer and not trail behind him (*see* Figs. 6 and 7). In teaching the colt to lead properly, a whip is used and the colt is taught not to fear it. Rather, he should regard it as an extension of the trainer's arm. Consequently, the whip *must not* be used for punishment.

The equipment used for longeing is simple. It consists of a longeing halter, a rope or webbing about thirty feet in length, and a longeing whip. This whip has a stock about four feet long and a lash of about twelve feet. It should be carried from the start so that the colt becomes accustomed to it. As the colt advances in his training he can be longed with a war bridle, or a longeing cavesson, a bosal, and finally with a bridle. Caution is necessary when longeing with the bridle for there is some danger of hurting the horse's mouth. (*See* Figs. 8, 9, 10, 11, and 12.)

Starting the horse on the longe line requires some patience as the horse does not know what he is expected to do. At this point, the horse has been taught to walk beside the trainer. Now he'll learn to go forward while the trainer gradually gets farther away from him. If a helper is available he can assist by walking behind the colt to keep him going forward until the colt will go freely by himself. If no helper is available the trainer should lead the young horse in a circle and gradually get farther away from him while using the lash of the whip to insure forward motion (*see* Fig. 13). The lash should be applied lightly to the colt's legs but not to the rump or croupe. It is best to keep walking with the colt, although in a smaller circle as the colt is accustomed to the trainer moving and tends to stop when he does. If the trainer is experiencing some trouble in maintaining forward motion in the colt he can help by walking near the colt's hip so that he is, in reality, driving the colt around the circle. (*See* Fig. 14.)

Until the colt will go forward freely and stay to the outside of the circle he should not be brought to the center. He should be stopped on the perimeter of the circle, standing there while the trainer pets him and encourages him with his voice. At this time it is wise to rub him

Figs. 6 and 7. Teach your horse to lead freely, walking beside you, not trailing behind.

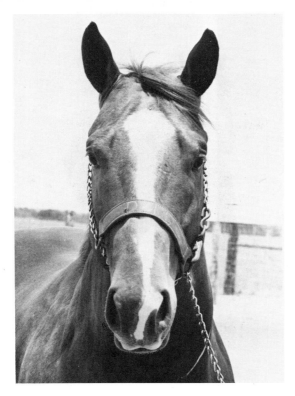

Fig. 8. The War bridle is one of the simplest
bridles.

Fig. 9. The War bridle is a good choice for beginning to longe the colt.

29

Fig. 10. Longe at the trot with halter.

Fig. 11. Longe with hackamore.

Fig. 12. Longe with snaffle.

Fig. 13. When longeing, use the whip only to insure forward motion.

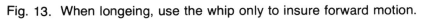

31

Fig. 14. If you have trouble maintaining forward motion, walk near the colt's hip to drive it forward and keep it moving.

Fig. 15. If the colt wants to run off some excess energy on the longe, let it!

with the folded whip so he does not fear it. Turn the colt to face the opposite direction. He won't go to the right as well as he does to the left since he is used to being led from the left side. A little patience and some kind words will get him going. He may turn back a few times and if he does, he should be stopped, turned, and started again in the right direction. Stand near his hip to help him start. It does not matter, at this time, whether he travels in a true circle, just keep him moving forward. It seems best to have him go in both directions the first day.

He should be allowed to walk for a few days until he learns to stop on command, to start, and go in both directions. He should not be worked until he is tired or sweating profusely—ten to fifteen minutes is long enough for the first few days.

The young horse, who has been kept in a stall and is full of grain, will usually want to run and play when first put on the line. Rather than stop him, it is best to let him work off his excess energy and then the lesson can be started. (*See* Fig. 15.)

During this time the horse is gaining confidence in his trainer and watching him very closely. The trainer must hold the longe line in his left hand when the horse goes to the left, or counterclockwise, and in his right hand to signal the horse to go to the right. The horse soon learns to watch the hand for the desired direction. By holding his arm straight out from his shoulder the trainer's signal is more easily recognized by the horse. (*See* Fig. 16.)

Verbal commands are taught to the horse while he is on the longe line. (*See* Fig. 17.) They should all be short—whoa, steady, walk, trot, lope, and come here—for horses cannot understand several words linked together although they may pick out one. The horse pays no attention to the expression on the trainer's face but he listens closely to his voice, and is encouraged by soft tones and alarmed at harsh commands.

The horse should be taught to stop on command. Say "whoa" (which many draw out to "whooooa") as this helps the horse to learn its meaning. Whoa can be taught by accompanying the command with a pull on the longe until he stops, at which time slack should be given immediately. Again, the trainer walks to the horse to let him know that he has obeyed.

When the horse stops and stands still he should be taught to come to the trainer in the center of the circle (*see* Fig. 18). This is very easy as it is much like the lesson he learned when taught to lead. This lesson is necessary in teaching the horse to work on the longe since the trainer has been driving him away.

Fig. 16. Teach the colt hand signals. Longe left with the line in the left hand, right with the line in the right hand. Hold the line at shoulder level to make the signal easily recognizable.

Fig. 17. This colt is stopped on the circle. Vocal commands—such as Whoa!—are taught on the longe line.

Fig. 18. "Come here." This is a good time to give the colt a confidence lesson. This is to teach the colt confidence in you, the trainer.

When the colt is brought to the trainer in the center of the circle he should be petted and vocally encouraged. Rub him with the whip, swing the end of the line over, under, and around him so he becomes accustomed to ropes around his legs and used to movement above him. This also presents an opportunity for him to rest a few minutes and gives the trainer a chance to pick up his feet. This can be called the confidence lesson. (*See* Figs. 19, 20, 21, and 22.)

Lightness of control is essential, so the longe line should have a curve or sag in it. In all of the horse's training, lightness must be a governing factor. He should not be hurried at the walk; this must be a natural gait and not an extended one. To walk naturally, the horse's head must be free. He needs to extend his neck, lower his head, and swing it up, down, and sideways.

All knowledgeable trainers agree that to develop balance, the horse must have a good trot. This is a gait of two-time to the horse; the rhythm is simple. He should trot easily with his head and neck held high. He is, naturally, in a state of partial collection with his hind feet farther under him than at the walk. This is the gait trainers prefer for much of their schooling. In this gait the horse does not tire as quickly, as in the lope or canter. Also, lead does not have to be considered, and the trainer need not follow with his hands, as the head and neck are relatively steady at the trot.

Fig. 19. Rub the colt with the whip.

Fig. 20. Swing the longe line over the colt.

Fig. 21. Pick up the colt's front feet.

Fig. 22. Pick up the colt's hind feet. This lesson will teach the colt not to fear handling or the longe equipment.

It is very easy to get a horse to trot while on the longe. The line should be reasonably loose to maintain lightness. His whole body should be in the arc of the circle in which he is traveling. His head must be to the inside. This will not happen if too much strain is placed on the lead. When held too highly, his head goes to the outside and he no longer travels on the arc of the circle but instead the colt will trot in a series of short, straight lines. He must not be forced or he will no longer go freely and enjoy his work.

The lope or canter should not be started on the longe until the horse is behaving nicely at the walk, trot, and stop.

When loose, he can go from the walk to the lope as easily as from the trot. He moves his leading hind leg under him and raises his head, collecting himself before loping. We cannot get him to do this on the longe but can only get him to go from the trot to the lope. If we could get him to lope at the exact time his trailing hind leg strikes the ground he would start on the correct lead but this is very difficult.

Starting him at the lope from the trot is best done when he is fresh so that he will not have to be forced into it. When forced to lope he will pull to the outside. A pull on the line, now, will throw his hindquarters to the outside, causing him to start on the wrong lead. (*See* Fig. 23.)

One of the greatest statements encountered in reading books on training is: "If laziness is the reason for a horse's failure to gallop, its dormant animation must be awakened by rigorous, inflammatory whip controls!" I hope you enjoy this line as much as I did when I first encountered it!

A good practice in longeing is to place some small objects, such as logs or poles, on the ground. This should be done from the first day. After the horse has been led over them a few times he no longer pays much attention to them. He soon starts to trot over them and when he is asked to lope over the poles he will select the correct lead. Within a couple of weeks he will walk, trot, or jump over them. When the colt will do this, the trainer will have gained his confidence and is giving him courage to do what is asked of him. (Those who are familiar with training hunters and jumpers know these logs or poles as a Cavaletti.) (*See* Figs. 24, 25, and 26.)

Not all horses are going to be trained as jumpers, but it does not hurt any horse to know how to jump; even our western horses are required to jump in trail horse classes. We can teach our horse to land on either lead while he is on the longe by pulling on it lightly while he is in the air. If we pull his head lightly to the left he will land on his left fore and so be on the left lead. This can be controlled from the horse's

Fig. 23. A colt at the lope on the longe. The lope should be started from a trot early in the lesson, when the horse is fresh.

Fig. 24. Place small objects on the ground and lead the horse over them. This exercise is known as a Cavaletti.

Fig. 25. After a few lessons the horse will lope over them, choosing the correct lead. These lessons teach the colt confidence in the trainer. The colt learns that the trainer will not ask him to do things he cannot do.

Fig. 26. Even a trail horse has to jump sometimes.

Fig. 27. Most horses, like these, are gentle.

Fig. 28. This colt is bitted with snaffle bit and side reins. When the colt is being gentled he should be saddled and bridled to become used to wearing the equipment.

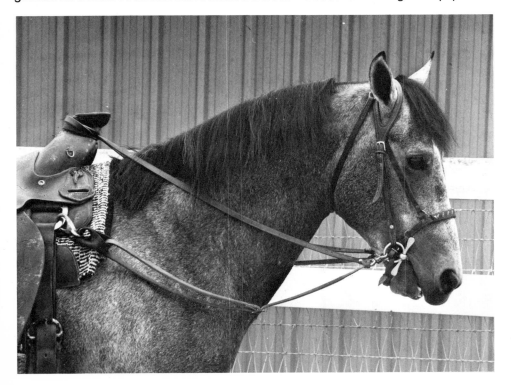

41

back by a gentle pull while he is in the air and is very important to a horse making a turn to go to the next jump. This system has been used for many years in Europe and especially in France.

Fortunately, most colts are reasonably gentle (*see* Fig. 27), though occasionally a wild one is encountered. Obviously, this wild colt will require more time, though the same methods will work. Until the colt is gentle, taught the oral commands, and longed on a loose line while saddled and bridled, he is not ready to ride. Some trainers believe this time is wasted but they are forgetting that colts ridden too soon acquire bad habits. This wild colt may have courage but he will not have any confidence or trust in a rider who has spurred, whipped, and ridden him by force.

Trotting or loping in small circles is an unnatural thing to ask a colt to do. A colt observed at play does not run in circles, unless they are very large circles. He runs, stops, turns around, and runs in a new direction. We are teaching the colt to work in circles with his head to the inside. This is often called following his head. In doing this, we have started lateral flexion which will be discussed in another chapter.

When the colt is gentle and is working reasonably well on the longe he should be saddled and bridled and allowed to become accustomed to this equipment while in his stall. Most trainers have one or two old saddles for this purpose. If the colt has been blanketed he seldom pays much attention to the saddle if he is not cinched too tightly. Most trainers prefer using a snaffle bit at this time as he will get used to leaning on the hackamore which must not be allowed. The reins are usually fastened to the saddle horn in such a way that there is no tension on them unless he lowers his head, or turns it sideways.

Many trainers like to use side reins in addition to the regular reins and this is a good practice. However, I believe the side reins should have some flexibility such as elastic or rubber in them. Side reins can be purchased at most saddleries, or a pair can be made by inserting a piece of inner tube. This does not teach the colt anything but it accustoms him to wearing the saddle and bridle. (*See* Fig. 28.) After being saddled in the stall for a half hour, he can be longed with the saddle and bridle on. The reins should be loose so they do not impair impulsion and the flopping of the stirrups accustoms him to the saddle.

When the colt will walk, trot, and lope both ways on a reasonably loose line he is ready to ride.

In conclusion it must be said that no matter what you teach on the longe line you will still have to teach it again when you ride the colt—but it will be much easier.

Chapter 3

Training Modern Methods

Horses and related wares are a $7 billion business! Figures released in 1969 by the American Horse Council and based on the reports of the U.S. Department of Agriculture prove that the horse business is a big business. The report stated that the horse population should exceed 10 million in 1977. Though the horse and mule population reached a high of 24 million during the peak of the "horse and buggy days" it dropped to a low of just under 3 million in 1959. This population explosion is having a significant impact on this leisure-time industry.

U.S.D.A. figures reflect that the *average* horse owner spends approximately $735 per-year per-horse on feed, equipment, tack, and drugs alone. There are over 500 major (plus many small) horse shows in the United States each year, plus horse activities at national, regional, and local livestock shows. Horse racing attracted over 65 million people in 1976—which is more than all professional and college football and baseball attendance combined! Further, the U.S.D.A. estimated that at least 82 million Americans rode a horse one or more times in 1977!

Interest in youth activities is growing; 4-H clubs, breed shows and open shows, and equitation classes are becoming more popular. This has created a demand for knowledgeable horse trainers who not only train the horse but also teach equitation.

The successful trainer is, in a sense, a perfectionist for he must have seemingly endless patience, as well as confidence in his ability. A good trainer is always searching for a better way of schooling, and an easier way of getting the horse to understand. He is never satisfied with his horse's performance; he believes he can improve it with more time. Perhaps the difference between a trainer and the pleasure rider can be explained by saying that when the trainer rides, he's working with his horse all the time he is on him, while the pleasure rider will work awhile and coast awhile. The rider coasting along with his legs hanging down is just a passenger. (*See* Fig. 29.)

Fig. 29. This rider is "just a passenger." Look at the legs.

This search for perfection in the horse's performance is horsemanship in the true sense of the word. Horsemanship can be defined as the
art, ability, skill, and manner of a horseman. The *art* lies in getting the
horse ready for advanced training by gaining his confidence, and
taking him through a program that advances step-by-step.

A trainer's ability may be measured by what he accomplishes, what
he wins, and how he does it. The trainer who uses fear as a training
method can never become popular, for horses trained by him are not a
pleasure to ride and in many cases they are not trained in such a way as
to be safe to ride. Some trainers believe that strength is the answer
and when this becomes the ruling force the horse is not light and
supple. He doesn't have a pleasing carriage or appearance. If strength
was the answer to horse training the strongest man would be the best
trainer. We know that this is not so. We even find that some of the best
trainers are physically handicapped.

The skill of a trainer can be gauged by his knowledge and compe-
tence, which can only come from experience. Nearly all successful
trainers admit that they made many mistakes when they first started

and that as the years passed they were forced to revise their training methods. The skillful trainer will encourage you to learn from your own experience by answering your questions in a roundabout way, and many times, just answering, "Well, it all depends."

You can tell the manner of a horseman by watching the way the horse regards his handler. If the horse is afraid or nervous in the presence of his trainer the method being used is not correct. The horse who considers his trainer a friend and shows this friendship by coming to be petted assures the onlooker that his handler's manner is acceptable.

Training methods have improved since the days of Xenophon, but the basic principles described by him still hold true. Two thousand years ago he instructed his students to change directions, so that the horse's jaws might be equally flexed. Xenophon taught horses patiently. He said that after mounting, the rider should sit still for more than the ordinary time.

It has been said that there is nothing new in equitation and perhaps this is so, for disputes as to the amount of flexion desirable in the horse were carried on in the sixteenth century just as they are today. Things we take for granted, such as the use of the longe line, were debated then. History records its use prior to the sixteenth century. With these statements we find mention of dressage, a study of the fine arts of riding.

Dressage is a word taken from the French and though there seems to be no exact translation of dressage into English, it means teaching an animal. However, this does not really define it, for it is believed to be more precisely defined as the art or ability to train a horse beyond the stage of plain usefulness.

Such famous horsemen as Comte d'Aure and Francois Baucher argued about training. Baucher maintained that the hand must always act before the leg, while d'Aure argued that the leg must act before the hand.

James Fillis, author of *Breaking and Riding*, studied Baucher and became a great exponent of Continental Horsemanship. The main object of his training was to produce a horse proficient in high-school work. He advocated extreme impulsion and collection.

The art of horsemanship has gone ahead since the days of Fillis. See for yourself in one of the best books on dressage today: *Dressage* by Henry Wynmalen. This book is well written and easy to read.

Just as the first step on the moon was a long one, the step from Xenophon to dressage was long. The step from novice horseman to accomplished horseman is also long, for the things to do and not to do are many. I do not believe in natural-born horsemen. I do believe that everyone who is physically fit can learn horsemanship, horse psychology, equitation, and showmanship if he will work and practice.

There can be no doubt that some people have a better sense of timing than others, some have better balance, some love horses, and some do not, but all can become proficient under a good trainer. Patience, experience, kindness, firmness, and a desire to continually improve the horse keep a trainer looking for the day he has the ideal horse. With a well-trained horse come other rewards (*see* Fig. 30).

When we speak of riding a horse we are in reality talking of equitation. When we consider equitation we find that it presents two problems: schooling the horse and teaching the rider.

Teaching the rider equitation must begin with how and where to sit in the western saddle. Some cutting horse riders believe that by sitting back against the cantle they help the horse to roll back over his hocks (*see* Fig. 31). The roper maintains that by standing in his stirrups he gets a better "throw" and helps his horse to stop, but some of the best riders position themselves as in Figs. 32, 33, 34, 35, and 36. The pleasure rider tries to sit in the center of his saddle to make his horse appear to ride easy. The reining horse rider moves around in his saddle to aid his horse in the difficult parts of the reining pattern.

We find that many ranchers and cowboys who can break a colt for ranch work and teach him to work stock do not know what a lead is and could not care less. Their horses are not a pleasure to ride and in many cases are dangerous. Their horses do not last for many years. The primary aim of a trainer should be to develop a horse to the best of its ability and to school it so it will last as long as possible.

After watching a countless number of rodeo cowboys ride, we must admit that very few of them sit a saddle. They stand in the stirrups, hang onto the horn, and balance on the reins. They do not claim to be good riders or horsemen and will admit that they just came to get the money.

These ranchers and cowboys will laugh at a youngster or an adult riding an English saddle but these English riders studied with an instructor and understand leads, diagonals, impulsion, flexion, and collection. (*See* Fig. 37.)

All horsemen hate change and the western rider is no exception. He seems to resent terms that are used in English riding and many Westerners think those who ride the flat saddle are sissies. They obviously have never played polo!

Fig. 30. The rider's reward comes with patience and a good horse.

Fig. 31. Chuck Olson demonstrates the cutting rider's belief that sitting back in the saddle helps the horse roll over his hocks.

Fig. 32. Matlock Rose works up front, moving around in the saddle trying to help the horse work.

Fig. 33. Roper Darrel Nickerson stands in his stirrups on R.O. Yesterday. Ropers maintain that standing in the stirrups gives them a better "throw" and enables them to help the horse stop.

Fig. 34. Buster Welch in his winning performance at the National Cutting Horse Championship on Rey Jay's Pete.

Fig. 35. Lanham Riley, a great roping horse trainer, shows his style on Ann's Patches.

Fig. 36. Dwight Stewart, cutting on the Champion of Champions, Major Thunder, demonstrates a well-balanced seat.

51

Fig. 37. Kathy Hastings shows the English way.

Trying to teach the novice how to ride has brought forth expressions such as, "the center of gravity," "the forward seat," and "the balanced ride." I question whether any of these expressions help the novice rider, since his primary problem is how to stay on the horse. Perhaps the best advice possible at this time is, "Keep one leg on each side of the horse and your mind in the middle." As he learns to ride he should understand that a horse carries more than half his weight on the forehand and that his hind legs propel him ahead. To help the horse, the rider should sit deep in the saddle, just behind the withers, and ride as though he were part of the horse and not something carried along on top. If the rider is sitting in the saddle properly he should be able to stand in his stirrups at the walk and lope without pulling on the reins or leaning forward.

If we agree that *confidence* is the most important word in training, then we must say that *impulsion* comes next. The horse can be likened to a boat in that the impulsion comes from the rear. A boat that is standing still cannot be steered; however, as soon as there is forward motion, the slightest movement of the tiller causes the boat to turn.

This applies to the horse for while he stands still he pays little attention to the reins but as soon as he starts forward he turns easily.

In all of his schooling, the horse must have forward motion—impulsion. He must be moving when he is being taught to turn. When he stops, so does the lesson and until we can get him going again the lesson cannot be resumed. This fact must be brought to the attention of the novice rider many times before he realizes its importance. We must also try to get the novice to understand horse psychology and apply it to the schooling of the horse.

Though it must be said that you cannot learn to ride by reading a book, Waldemar Seunig remarked in his excellent book, *Horsemanship* (1961): "Books do not make a rider good or bad but they can make him better or worse."

Chapter 4

Riding the Green Colt

Fortunately, today most colts that are sent to a trainer are reasonably gentle. They have been raised in a pasture or small paddock and handled and gentled as they grew. These gentle colts need none of the cruel breaking methods used on wild horses. Tying up a colt's foot or blindfolding him and letting him buck is unnecessary and dangerous.

The colt we are going to ride has been trained on the longe line, saddled and bitted in his stall, and longed with the equipment on him. He has been taught obedience, oral commands, and confidence in his trainer while on the longe.

Begin schooling the colt in a small enclosure, such as a large stall or a small corral or breaking ring. This is a suitable place in which to teach the colt to allow the rider to mount and dismount (*see* Fig. 38). The colt must be taught to stand quietly while this is done. If his previous lessons were properly taught he will seldom give you any trouble about being mounted. Of course, care should be taken not to startle him by quick movements (*see* Fig. 39). The rider should ease quietly into the saddle talking to the colt all the while. Pet him if he stands still. Get on and off many times and from both sides until the colt is thoroughly accustomed to this procedure. While you're sitting on the colt, swing the ends of the reins above him. This will accustom him to movement above him. (*See* Fig. 40.)

This time is well spent, for all through his life this colt will be expected to stand quietly while being mounted. If he goes to the shows, he must stand still for the rules stipulate it. To insure his standing still when being mounted it is best to sit still a little while after mounting. As Xenophon so nicely said: "After mounting, the rider should sit quiet more than the ordinary time."

When the colt becomes accustomed to the sight and feel of someone on his back he must be taught to go forward and to walk around the enclosure. He will need some urging at first, for he will not want to move. With the use of certain aids—the rider's voice and legs—the colt

Fig. 38. Begin riding in a small enclosure—a large stall, a corral, or a breaking ring.

Fig. 39. Mount the green colt gently, talking quietly. Take care not to startle the colt.

Fig. 40. Swing the end of the reins to accustom the colt to movement above it.

Fig. 41. The green colt may carry its head low. This is natural; don't try to raise it.

can be started. The impulsion that drives him ahead and keeps him going must come from the rider's legs and heels only. Spurs should never be worn on a young horse.

As soon as the colt has accepted the rider he can be taken to the ring or corral in which he will be trained. There he can be taught to walk freely. A good walk is the basis of his future development and is difficult to teach.

The green colt will usually walk with his head low and his neck extended. This is proper at the beginning of his training. The rider should not pull hard enough on the reins to flex the jaw or raise the head (*see* Fig. 41). The colt should be stopped frequently and allowed to stand for at least thirty seconds (*see* Fig. 42).

After each stop and short rest the colt must be started again. The lesson to be taught is that he must go forward freely at the touch of the rider's leg. The rider's voice and legs will accomplish this. Take care not to startle the colt by squeezing too hard or too near the flanks. The colt will soon learn that the leg aid is a signal to go forward. When this happens the verbal commands can be discontinued.

Fig. 42. Many trainers begin riding the green colt with snaffle bridle and bosalito. The green colt should be stopped and allowed to stand often in the early lessons.

Most trainers prefer to start the colt with the snaffle bit (*see* Fig. 43) even though they intend to ride him with the hackamore. A week in the snaffle and then a switch to the hackamore is common practice. This seems best as there is less chance of skinning his lower jaw with the hackamore once the chances of his becoming startled are less. Many believe the snaffle used with a running martingale helps to control the green colt. (*See* Figs. 44 and 45.)

The argument of the snaffle versus the hackamore will probably never be settled; the advocates of each are many and firm in their opinions. Fine results have been accomplished by both methods and I think that the one that works best for you is the one you should use.

The horse carries his head lower at the walk and gallop than he does at the trot or lope. At every stride of the walk and lope his head swings backward and forward. This helps his movements just as the swinging of his arms helps a man. Also, at the walk there is some sideways swinging of the head. At the trot the head and neck no longer swing. To walk fast the horse's head must be free.

The rider must keep light contact with the horse's mouth through the reins for he must teach the colt to travel straight at the walk and the trot. The colt must travel with his head and neck straight in front of his body. Equally important, his hind legs must travel straight behind his forelegs. (*See* Fig. 46.)

The rider must remember that whether the snaffle bridle or hackamore is being used, they must be ridden with a rein in each hand. Neither is intended for riding with one hand, especially at this point in the horse's training. (*See* Fig. 47.)

During these first few days of the colt's schooling he should not be asked to make quick stops or sudden changes of gait. The colt is ready to be ridden in the pasture if he will stop when the rider says "Whoa," while pulling gently on the reins. The rider must be careful not to pull hard enough to flex the lower jaw or raise the head. Each stop should be followed by about thirty seconds of standing still.

We must always be sure that when going at the faster gaits we can slow the colt or stop him. A few days of going slowly will be well spent as the colt becomes manageable and learns to give to the bit. Many trainers use a running martingale at this time; when riding in the pasture something may frighten the colt and without the martingale he can throw his head up and become uncontrollable.

I have often used the running martingale and I can see nothing wrong with its use, provided it is used on the snaffle rein and not on the curb rein.

Fig. 43. Riding the colt with snaffle bridle. Trainers often start the colt in a snaffle bridle rather than the hackamore as there is less chance of skinning the colt's lower jaw in a snaffle bridle.

Fig. 44. Colt with snaffle bridle, bosalito, and running martingale. The bosalito and running martingale help control the colt in his early training. They insure that the colt can't get his head out of control.

Fig. 45. A green colt being trained in snaffle bridle and hackamore.

Fig. 46. The colt must be taught to travel straight. Head and neck should be straight in front of the body, the hind legs straight behind the fore legs.

How fast training may progress depends on the rider's proficiency and on each individual colt. The accomplished trainer is the one who can tell when the colt has learned the lesson being taught and is ready for the next. Trainers know that to teach an utter novice how to ride an untrained horse is an almost hopeless task. Conversely, for the novice to undertake the training of a green colt is futile.

When the colt is going calmly at the walk and trot he can be galloped. The colt is galloped before he's loped because the lope must be taught. This should be done in a corral or ring since the trainer can control the colt better in a ring or large corral. There the fences help teach the colt to turn. Also, the fences can be used as an aid in getting him to gallop on the correct lead. He must go from the trot to the gallop at this time, and, just as he is approaching a corner, he is allowed to change gaits; the turn will usually put him on the correct lead. Although he may be going faster than desired, it is best to let him do so, provided the rider can guide and stop him at will. Here, again, we are concerned with impulsion. We must get him to gallop by leg pressure and the use of the voice, so it is best not to try to slow him at this time.

There is some increased tension on the reins at the gallop, though it is very important to allow the colt's head to move forward and backward. The rider's hands must give and take with the swinging of the head while maintaining this tension. There must be continuous contact since a loose swinging rein does not steady the colt; instead, he becomes nervous. Always remember that the faster a horse goes the more he must be supported by the reins.

The colt's conduct will tell when he is ready for more advanced training. When he begins to take hold of the bit as he becomes stronger, start teaching him to relax his lower jaw and to bend his neck. This lesson develops the head carriage the horse must have. This is often called *finish*.

We have three things to teach: relaxing the lower jaw so that he will open his mouth just a little at a pull stronger than usual, bending his neck sideways (called lateral flexion), and flexing at the poll (called vertical flexion).

Westerners resent the terms and expressions used in English riding. Flexion, suppleness, collection, and impulsion seem to raise specters of the double bridle and flat saddle. Flat saddle riders are not the sissies some think. Polo, played on flat saddles, is a game only for the hardy, as is the steeplechase. It must be admitted that you cannot rope a steer or ride a cutting horse with a flat saddle. Conversely, you cannot successfully clear a five-foot-high jump or show a horse in three-day events in a western saddle. All horsemen hate change but change is the only thing that has brought progress.

This is not an attempt to get you to ride and train on a flat saddle. Rather I want to emphasize the importance of proper control of the horse's head through the reins and control of his quarters by correct use of the rider's legs. The difference between riding a stiff-necked horse and one that is light and supple is as great as that between driving a semi-trailer truck and a Coupe de Ville with power steering.

Flexions do not all come at once and lateral flexion must be taught before vertical. Fortunately while we are teaching lateral flexion the horse is also beginning to flex vertically. (*See* Fig. 49.)

This training can best be done at the trot for at that gait the horse's head and neck remain still and he naturally carries it higher than at the walk or gallop. In reality, at this gait, he is partially collected and more mobile. By trotting the colt in many small circles and figure eights while using the leading rein, you begin to teach him to follow his head. By this we mean that as he goes in a circle his head must be to the inside and his neck and back curved in the arc of the circle. It is not

Fig. 49. Lateral flexion, start of vertical flexion. The lateral flexion is seen in the neck, turned sideways; the vertical in the flexing at the poll. This is called *finish*.

natural for a horse to go in small circles but your work on the longe will have prepared him for this and added impulsion from the rider's legs will keep him going.

The rider's hands are completely responsible for teaching the colt to relax his jaw. At this time his jaw should open easily but only a little way; there should be no wide opening of the mouth, called *gaping*. The colt should close his mouth when the pressure from the reins lessens. Often he will chew once or twice after he closes his mouth and this is as it should be. The rider must feel this relaxing of the jaw and reward the colt for this by giving slack on the reins. This must be done every time and as quickly as possible. This giving of slack as a reward for obedience is called *tact*.

All horses resent a steady pull and so in teaching lateral flexion the rider cultivates a soft mouth by little light pulls and releases on the reins. The rider pulls the horse's head to the inside as he trots in a circle and releases it. The horse straightens out his neck and the rider puts it back to the inside. This is done over and over again while trotting in the circles and figure eights. Pulling the horse's head to the inside and holding it there is just not done.

Fig. 50. Marilyn Hite demonstrates an over-flexed leading rein on The Globe Master.

There is the danger of over-flexion, both lateral and vertical (*see* Fig. 50). This must be avoided as the horse becomes unmanageable when over-flexed because he gets his head back of vertical and several bad things begin to happen. He lowers his head, nervous, jigs instead of walks, and is inclined to run away when galloping. With his head in against his chest the horse develops a defense against the bit and cannot be taught to stop and slide when he puts his head down.

The control of the horse's head can be accomplished only by proper use of the rider's hands. You'll hear good riders described as having "warm hands," "live hands," or "following hands." The finished trainer must acquire hands that give and take, and that maintain a constant light contact with the horse's mouth with just enough pressure to control his head. Always remember, it's all in the hands.

As the training in this phase of the colt's development progresses, the rider can feel lightness of balance and willingness to accept the bit. Also, the colt's head has been gradually getting higher. The exercises with the leading rein and the flexions have moderated the stiffness of his neck. The rider's hands regulate the height of the head. The western horse should carry his head so that his eyes are about the same height as his withers. This gives him an alert and attractive appearance and also aids his balance.

Conformation must be considered in training. We find that the horse with the short or heavy neck usually has a broad chest and cannot become as light and supple as one with more desirable characteristics. The horse with the short, heavy neck can only flex slightly at the poll before he becomes uncomfortable, even to the point of having trouble breathing properly.

As the colt progresses in his training with the leading rein we begin to gradually bring the hand closer to his neck until we are using the direct rein. This must be done in preparation for the day when he will be ridden one-handed and neck-reined. However, there should be no attempt at this time to teach him to give to the bearing rein or neck rein.

Rein control can never be reliable unless based on leg control. We know that the colt must go forward willingly at a squeeze from the rider's legs but this is only one part of leg control. As the colt goes in a circle, more pressure is needed from the rider's outside leg than from the inside leg. This aids in keeping the colt on the circle. Each time we change direction we must change leg pressure. When turning to the left with the left rein, the right leg assists. When going to the right, the left leg takes over. We must learn to ride both ends of the horse, for it is impossible to ride a horse straight by the use of the reins only, just as it is impossible to turn a green horse on the hind legs by the reins alone.

The hackamore, that controversial piece of equipment favored by trainers on the west coast, is of Spanish origin and is la jáqima in that language. The braided, rawhide nose band is called the bosál and the hair reins the mecáte. On some hackamores there is an added piece called the fiadore, attached to the heel knot and fastened around the horse's neck so that he may be tied with the hackamore without the bosál being slipped off his chin by a pull from the front.

All things done with the snaffle bit, with the exception of relaxing the lower jaw, can be done with the hackamore. The lateral and vertical flexions can be taught and lightness is possibly its most outstanding accomplishment. However, use of the hackamore requires understanding of its principles for it differs from the snaffle in several ways. As mentioned before, it is a two-handed instrument and was never intended to be used with one hand only.

The hackamore reinsman tries to school his colt so that he does not use two reins at the same time and so, great emphasis is placed on the give and take of the reins, even to a little seesaw motion as preferred over a steady pull with both reins. The height of the horse's head is controlled by the hands. The leading rein and the direct rein are handled much the same as with the snaffle.

The colt must not be bitted in his stall with the hackamore. He may get in the habit of resting his head too heavily on it. Before riding, he is bitted with a snaffle or a light curb bit which is replaced by the hackamore when he is ridden. (*See* Fig. 51.)

Not all trainers believe in bitting the colt in the stall before riding but I have done so for many years and believe it helps in several ways. While bitting probably does not teach the colt much, it does accustom him to the bridle and he finds that he cannot get away from the bit. He is also used to the saddle and is not so inclined to be "cold-backed" when the rider mounts. The use of side reins is beneficial but some elastic or a piece of old inner tube used with them is good for it gives them a little stretch. They seem to aid the vertical flexion at the poll, and I can see no harm in using them. (*See* Fig. 52.)

Some trainers believe that the colt is best saddled and ridden without bitting and as the colt advances in his training this can be done without any problem. The busy trainer gains some time by the bitting, for the colt is more relaxed and will start the lesson sooner than the colt just saddled and ridden. Those who have a mechanical horse-

Fig. 51. Before the lesson, the colt is bitted with curb bit and bosalito. The bridle will be removed and the lesson given with a hackamore.

Fig. 52. This colt has been bitted with curb and side reins before a lesson. This accustoms the colt to the bridle and teaches him that he can't get away from the bit.

Fig. 53. These colts are on a mechanical walker. This saves the trainer time; they will be more relaxed for the lesson.

walker often put the colt on it for half-an-hour before riding which helps get him ready for the lesson, especially if he is saddled at that time. (*See* Fig. 53.)

Whether the colt is ridden with the snaffle or the hackamore, or as some do, alternating between them, the trot is the trainer's gait. In the little circles and small figure eights the colt learns to go forward freely, to give to the leading rein and then the direct rein, to respond to the pressure of the rider's leg at each change of direction, to gallop, and, finally, lope on the correct lead, while going in large circles. No attempt should be made, at this point in the horse's training, to teach the flying change of leads.

The colt that was started on the longe line will lope in a circle and if allowed to trot into the lope will select the correct lead. No attempt to lope from the walk should be made at this stage and many trainers post the trot to help the colt select the correct lead. To do this the rider should rise in time with the forearm of the colt on the outside of the circle. Thus, going to the left the rider should rise with the colt's right forearm.

When loping the colt in a circle it is best to trot him a few steps before changing direction and then lope as in the following diagram. While doing this the colt is learning to lope with his head to the inside of the circle, to trot straight from one point to another, and to lope when the reins are loosened. The size of the circles and the distance between them can be varied but a circle forty to fifty feet in diameter is a good size. The circles should be separated as though there were another circle between them.

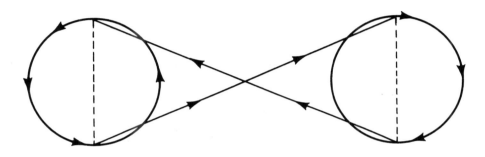

Fig. 54. The Dressage Figure Eight is an excellent teaching pattern for the lope and the trot.

For want of a better name I have called this figure the Dressage Figure Eight. Its value and use in teaching the flying change of leads will be discussed in another chapter. Fortunately, this figure can be ridden many times without the horse becoming sour or ring-wise provided you vary the number of times you go around the circle. Two times around and then cross over is better than once around. We must keep the horse from starting across each time he comes to the spot at which he leaves the circle for all horses are quick to pick up a routine. The dotted lines bisecting the circle are only imaginary but they indicate the place at which we leave or enter the circle.

Riding this pattern is fine training for beginners. It teaches the rider to work his hands and reins together with his legs. To ride the X in a straight line is not as simple as it appears for the horse does not naturally travel straight. He can only be ridden straight by controlling his head and neck through the reins and the hindquarters by the use of the rider's legs. In addition, the rider should pick out a spot to ride to or he will find he is riding in a crooked line. At the spot where the X intersects the circle the horse should lope and he should trot at the point where the X leaves the circle.

As the horse trots across the X the rider must increase his leg pressure to the point that the horse wants to lope as he reaches the circle. Then, instead of pulling his head to the inside, the rider loosens the outside rein, at which time the horse must lope. This increase of impulsion is very important. This is a base for advanced training that the colt will receive later.

When the colt performs quietly and reliably on this figure he is ready for the next lesson, the push-off, where he will learn the shoulder-in, the two-track, and the sidepass.

Chapter 5
The Push-off

When the colt has progressed from the leading rein to the direct rein and has acquired some lateral flexion, work on two-tracks should be started. From this comes the push-off and the shoulder-in which leads to the sidepass. This sounds very complex but on two-tracks simply refers to the movements in which a horse's forefeet and hind feet travel in different tracks, as in the sidepass. The push-off or shoulder-in must be done with the head and neck flexed to the *opposite* direction to which the horse goes, and his body must be at an angle of from thirty to forty-five degrees *with* the direction in which he is going. (*See* Figs. 55 and 56.)

At the start, the angle is unimportant as there will be some difficulty encountered in getting the colt to go sideways at any angle. Not only does he dislike doing this, but it is also difficult for him. It is not natural for a horse to move sideways. Additionally, a horse does not have ball and socket joints in his legs as we have in our hips. To move to the side he must cross his legs. He does not want to do any of these things.

We have spent a great deal of time teaching our colt to work in circles and this has helped to increase the horse's flexibility. All the sideways movements of the horse are learned in the circle and as he goes around it we push him off the outside of the circle by pressure from the rider's inside leg. At the same time, the rider moves his hands in the direction of the push-off.

Let us assume we are going around a circle to the left, with the colt's head and neck flexed to the inside. We have been taught to use pressure from the rider's leg on the outside of the circle to create impulsion and to prevent the horse from swinging his quarters to the outside. Also, we have been instructed to use the direct rein to turn the colt and to lengthen the outside rein, or indirect rein, to aid him in bending his neck while not impeding impulsion. It cannot be overemphasized that he must go forward *freely*.

Fig. 55. Jane Hastings demonstrates the push-off
with front legs crossing on R.O. Major Dandy.

Although we discussed the riding of circles in Chapter 4, it
seems best to talk about this exercise again, because if the circles are
not ridden properly the push-off will not work.

Imagine that you are riding the colt in a straight line with a rein in
each hand, and with the same tension on each rein; the colt is going
forward freely. To start in a circle, we do not pull harder with the
inside rein, instead, loosen the outside or indirect rein. This is a fine
distinction but an important one. It is exactly what you should do in
the Dressage Figure Eight at the time the colt goes from the trot to
the lope.

On a large circle we have very little difficulty but on a small one we
must have more lateral flexion of the neck and so must increase our
impulsion. We are also teaching the colt collection, relaxation of his
lower jaw, and turning his head to the side. Flexions are more easily
obtained by the use of one rein rather than two, so we are obtaining
some flexion at the poll, also. Our western horse needs to be taught
semi-collection only; he does not require complete collection.

Fig. 56. This is the push-off with hind legs crossing.

The push-off, called the shoulder-in in dressage, is best taught from the circle with which both the rider and the horse are now familiar. Let us assume we are riding in a small circle going to the left. We are using the left rein as a direct rein and the right leg for impulsion and control of the colt's hindquarters. We push him off the outside of the circle by changing to pressure of the inside leg, in this case the left one. At the same time we move both of our hands to the right or in the direction of the push-off.

We must maintain lateral flexion and forward motion or he will not push off. Remember this is not a natural action for the colt and he does does not want to go sideways. He will probably do one of two things wrong: stop or straighten out his neck. If either of these things happen we must start forward again, get back on the circle, flex him to the inside, and try again. We make it as easy for him as possible by trying for a lot of forward motion and only a little sideways motion. At even a suggestion of sideways movement we must encourage the colt vocally and by petting. This is a difficult lesson and the rider must control any inclination to lose his temper.

The accompanying diagram shows the desired position of the horse as he pushes off. This is also called the shoulder-in and is the only movement on two-tracks where the horse is flexed away from the direction in which he is going (*see* Fig. 57). This appears to be easy, but it is much more difficult than it seems to be. However, it is one of the most important lessons. Both rider and horse need to master this, so be patient!

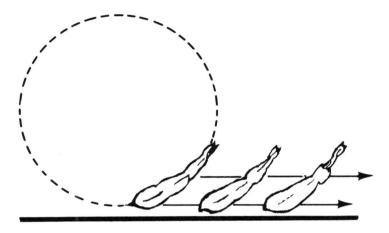

Fig. 57. The push-off away from the direction in which the horse is travelling is called the shoulder-in.

The push-off has great value to the show horse. He is required to sidepass in trail horse classes and working cowhorse classes. Additionally, it serves as a means of controlling a horse in the open, in negotiating gates, and has great value in finishing the reined horse. All of these things will be discussed in detail in another chapter.

I prefer to teach the push-off in the center of the ring, or at least away from any fences; the practice of heading a horse into a fence and spurring him in the side to make him sidepass is harmful. This is essentially an exercise of forward motion and anything that tends to hinder his going forward is contrary to good horsemanship and good training.

Remember, everything must be just right or it will not work: the head and neck position and the forward movement are musts. It is not hard to teach when the rider has mastered his part. The hackamore is more than adequate for teaching the push-off.

Chapter 6
The Bearing Rein

Most of us who were raised on a ranch never heard of the bearing rein. Until we began to enter horse shows and learn the names and expressions used in teaching horses to become more than just a riding horse, the neck rein was our way of guiding the horse. Perhaps it isn't necessary for the rider who is satisfied with a horse that will turn at the pressure of the rein against his neck to understand that this method of reining is often called the bearing rein, the outside rein, the indirect rein, or the rein of opposition. However, I believe that any knowledgeable horseman will be interested in these terms and want to know what they mean and how they are used.

We have talked about the leading rein, the open rein, and the direct rein. In those references we are speaking of the inside rein. Now we are going to work with the outside rein, the one that *bears* against the horse's neck and which we will call the bearing rein.

I have never been able to find when it was first used or by whom, but history tells us that it was prior to the conquest of Spain by the Moors.

When this occurred the Spaniards were riding horses of European breeding. These horses were ridden with a rein in each hand just as horses ridden today with English equipment are. When the Spanish cavalaryman engaged in a fight he was forced to drop his reins on his horse's neck to wield his heavy sword.

This was not so with the Moors who were riding horses of Barb and Arab cross. These horses were faster and quicker than the Spanish horses. They were ridden with one hand, leaving the rider's right hand free to fight with his curved sword. While history doesn't tell us that these horses were neck-reined it seems safe for us to assume that they were. These differences in the horses and the two armies' ways of riding are sometimes given as reasons for the Moors' conquest of Spain.

The Moors ruled Spain for about seven hundred years until the Spaniards revolted. During this time the Spaniards accepted the

Moorish manner of riding and their equipment. From this came the equipment, the manner of riding, and the training methods brought to Mexico by the Conquistadors many years later.

The bearing rein is the third and last of the basic lessons the horse must master. Riding in circles is the most important exercise the young horse must master. There are many effects that come from riding in circles. These include flexibility, suppleness, and balance. There are many good reasons for riding in circles. The lateral flexion of the colt's neck can be taught from his back without resorting to the exercises from the ground as once recommended by Fillis and Baucher. In working from his back there isn't much chance of the over-flexion that occurs when these exercises are taught from the ground.

The question of whether the western horse needs collection or not has never been settled. Some believe he goes best with his head low and his nose pointed out in front of him in what we might call "ant-eater" style. (See Fig. 58.)

There can be no doubt that the horse negotiates rough terrain better if he has his head free. If the horse is able to raise or lower it he can see and balance better. But, is this the way we want a horse to travel in the show ring?

I want to say that show business is show business and appearance must be considered. The judge makes his placings from what he sees in the ring and few people can say that a horse presents a more pleasing appearance traveling with his head low in a lazy, shambling way.

If we agree that a horse presents a better appearance traveling with his head up and his neck bent at the poll we must have collection and with this must come a relaxing of the horse's lower jaw. Usually a horse who will relax his jaw opens his mouth just a little. This is as it should be (see Figs. 59 and 60). However, this is not the wide open mouth we see when the horse who is behind the bit is suddenly bumped with it for a stop.

We must remember that the horse can't turn without his hind legs well under him, neither can he make the long slide and stop under any other condition. When the horse flexes correctly he will be light and rein easily.

With the exception of relaxing the jaw, all this can be taught with the hackamore. The hackamore reinsman believes that after the horse has become light and supple in the hackamore the transition from it to the bridle is a simple one and the horse soon accepts the bit and relaxes his jaw.

Fig. 58. No collection—Sissy Bars Chock carries her head too low. (Chris Cason up.)

Fig. 59. Collection at the trot, head held high, and the neck bent at the poll presents a much more pleasing appearance.

Fig. 60. Collection on the rail at the lope. Collection is necessary for the horse needs his hindquarters well under him for advanced maneuvers.

The use of the hackamore and its training principles was a well-kept secret of the Californians for many years. The method of using it was passed on from father to son and from friend to close friend. Nothing was written about it until 1952 at which time Ed Connel produced a very fine work, *The Hackamore Reinsman*, that is ably illustrated by Randy Steffen. It is well worth reading by anyone interested in the ways of the California Dons.

The secret of this method of training lies in the way the reins are handled, for the horse learns to work properly by continuous repetition of the use of the reins and becomes very light in the hackamore. Differences of opinion exist between those who prefer the California way and those who advocate the Texas style of training with a snaffle bridle and grazer bit. The beauty of hackamore training lies in the fact that when the hackamore horse is ready for the bridle he can be worked in any kind of curbed bit or spade bit, for he has learned to handle himself in the hackamore. Many trainers believe the best all-around horses are made with the old-time methods.

The hackamore reinsman must have a light hand. The light pulls while giving slack is the basic principle used by him. He tries to avoid the steady pull or the pulling of both reins at the same time.

The mecáte (may-cót-tay), the hair rope used for reins and lead, is not popular with some riders as it is prickly to soft hands. However, it is made to attract the horse's attention to its pressure against his neck; he soon gives to the light touch of this hair rope. It is a great asset in teaching the bearing rein. (*See* Fig. 61.)

When the hackamore horse advances in his training he is bitted in his stall with a curb bit and side reins (*see* Fig. 62). Thus, he becomes accustomed to the bit long before he is ridden with it. When the trainer feels that the horse is ready for advanced training and work in the bridle, he rides the horse with a light hackamore under the bridle. While he is really riding with four reins this is called two-reining or riding a horse "straight up" (*see* Fig. 63). The bridle reins are used very lightly and the hackamore assists. Gradually the hackamore is used less and less until the horse can be handled lightly in the bridle. This is the old California system and with it, many of the great reined horses were made.

Today, we find many western trainers who use a full bridle for training. (*See* Fig. 64.) This use of the snaffle and curb bit or bit and bridoon with the two reins gets a very similar result to riding straight up.

It seems wise to again discuss how we ride a horse as we start him in a circle. First we start him straight ahead with light contact with his mouth through the reins and light leg pressure to insure impulsion. Many riders, when they wish to start the circle, pull with the direct rein to turn the horse. This does two things that are bad! It holds him back and he cannot turn his head in the arc of the circle until the outside rein is loosened. A better way to start him in the circle is to loosen the outside rein and he will then follow the direct rein and go with his head, neck, and body properly flexed.

When we consider how a horse turns of his own accord we find that as he turns to the left he swings his hindquarters to the right and turns mainly on his front legs. The forehand acts as a pivot and his quarters walk around this pivot in a large circle. Try this on your horse while leading him and you will find that this is the way he prefers to turn. From this we learn that to make the horse turn on his hind legs he must be held back by the halter or bridle.

This same problem arises with the partially trained horse as he is ridden in a circle; he tends to go to the outside because he doesn't want to travel in circles. When the rider pulls his head to the inside, with the inside, leading, open, or direct rein, he throws the horse's hindquarters to the outside. This must not be done as the horse progresses in

Fig. 61. The hackamore can teach everything the snaffle bit does except relaxation of the lower jaw. Hackamore reinsmen believe lightness is the outstanding asset of the hackamore-trained horse.

Fig. 62. As the hackamore horse advances in his training he is bitted with curb bit and side reins in his stall to accustom him to this equipment.

Fig. 63. "Two-reining" or riding a horse "straight up" with light hackamore under a bridle occurs when the trainer thinks the horse is ready for more advanced training. The bridle reins will be used lightly at first and will gradually replace the hackamore as the controlling agents.

Fig. 64. A full bridle gets a similar result to riding "straight up" and many western trainers are using it today.

his training. The bearing rein begins to assist in keeping the horse on the circle and it is accompanied by stronger pressure from the rider's leg, which is on the outside of the circle. (*See* Fig. 65.)

Riding with two hands is best for this schooling. The horse's head must be to the inside and the rider must maintain impulsion by vigorous leg pressure. If the colt still doesn't neck rein, he soon will if you use your hands properly. In fact, you can't keep him from it!

The hands must travel together in such a way that they are never more than six inches apart. The bearing rein is against his neck and the direct rein aids in enforcing the turn. In doing this, both hands often seem to be on the same side of the horn but this must not be allowed. The hand holding the bearing rein may be above the horn but not beyond it. The rider must remember that the horse will soon be ridden with one hand and the reins will then travel together. He is attempting to get this same action with a rein in each hand plus putting a tremor or vibration in the bearing rein to call the horse's attention to it. (*See* Fig. 66.)

There must be a give and take with the rider's hands. As the horse travels in a circle with his head to the inside, the rider must let the hand holding the outside rein go forward so that there is the same tension on both reins. Each time the rider changes direction the hands must change and the hand holding the bearing rein must go up and above the horn. (*See* Fig. 67.)

Before training the horse to respond to the bearing rein our emphasis has been on the inside rein, but now it must be transferred to the outside or bearing rein. When the outside or bearing rein bears against the horse's neck, call his attention to it with a tremor or a vibration. This movement of the rein must not be hard enough to be called a jerk. It should not impede the impulsion. If the horse does not respond to this rein and turn as desired, use the direct rein. This direct rein must *not* maintain a steady pressure; just pull and give slack. The horse will quickly learn that he must respond to the bearing rein. When the reins are handled in this manner you can't keep him from neck reining. (*See* Fig. 68.)

There is no magic formula or shortcut to training a horse. Successful trainers must have infinite patience because many young horses are spoiled by someone trying to teach them too rapidly and working them too long at each lesson. Colts do better when ridden every day and for not more than an hour at one time. Some colts are eager to please and these colts must be carefully schooled for they learn bad habits as quickly and as well as good ones.

Fig. 65. Marilyn Hite riding The Globe Master with bearing rein, circles with the hackamore.

Fig. 66. When teaching the bearing rein, the hands should move together never more than six inches apart.

Fig. 67. Marilyn Hite shows correct hand position on R.O. Major Dandy. When the hands are right, the head will be too.

Fig. 68. The neck rein bears against the horse's neck. It is also known as the bearing rein.

Fig. 69. The horse's head is too high because the rider's hands are too high.

Fig. 70. The horse's head is too low. The rider has no contact with the horse's mouth.

Fig. 71. When you have correct hand position, correct head position will follow.

The horse's head is controlled by the rider's hands. If the hands are too high or too low, so is the horse's head. This also means that if the rider's hands are in the correct position, the horse's head will be, also. (*See* Figs. 69, 70, and 71.)

Chapter 7

The Gaits of the Horse

The advanced horseman must understand the rhythm of the horse's gaits. This rhythm of action is a topic men have argued about for hundreds of years. History tells us that the ancient Egyptians debated whether the trotting horse ever had all four legs off the ground at the same time, for the human eye cannot stop the horse's action and tell exactly what takes place. So, it is no wonder that the canter, lope, and gallop are confusing when the trot, the simplest gait of the horse, is not fully understood.

Around 1872, Leland Stanford arranged with a photographer, Eadweard Muybridge, to take pictures of the horse in action. What seemed simple turned out to be very difficult. Muybridge started with one camera, then tried a battery of twelve cameras, and finally used twenty-four cameras. He spent ten years on these experiments. In 1882 he published his classic study, *The Horse in Motion*.

The pictures taken by Eadweard Muybridge showed that the artists of the day were not correct and the conclusions of horsemen were incorrect, also. This was due to the fact that the horse's action is a sequence of complicated movements and the rider causes irregularities in these. These movements of the horse were not clearly defined until the movie camera came along.

Today, we know that the walk is a relaxed gait. The horse must have freedom of his head to swing it up, down, and sideways. His head and neck should be well out in front of him and allowed to swing in time with the movements of his legs. There should be very little contact with his mouth through the reins and bit. He must have freedom of his head to walk fast. The walk is a pace or gait of four-time, as each foot moves individually and strikes the ground at regular intervals. Beginning with the near hind, the legs move near hind, near fore, off hind, and off fore. There are always at least two feet on the ground. Almost invariably the horse that is standing still will move a hind foot first as he starts to walk. (*See* Figs. 72, 73, 74, and 75.)

Fig. 72. The walk usually begins with a hind foot—here the right hind.

Fig. 73. Right fore follows. There are always two feet on the ground.

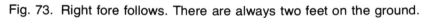

Fig. 74. Left hind. The walk is a four-time gait of regular intervals.

Fig. 75. Left fore. The horse's head and neck should be well in front of him and allowed (as shown) to swing in time with his leg movements.

Most of the forward push, or impulsion, comes from the horse's hind legs as the rider's legs drive him ahead. The forward push starts when the horse's hind leg is nearly perpendicular. Pressure from the calf of the rider's leg, then, will cause the horse to push a little harder with that leg. As the horse's near hind is straight up and down, the rider squeezes with his left leg and then his right as the off hind is perpendicular, making the horse push harder and walk faster. Thus, the expression, "the rider walks with his horse."

The trot is a two-time gait. It is a natural gait and should not be confused with the jog-trot, a man-given, or artificial, gait. In both the trot and the jog-trot, the diagonal legs move together as a pair. Since two legs move together, this gait is often said to be in two-four time. Thus, the near hind and off fore move together and then the off hind and near fore together (*see* Figs. 76 and 77). The trot differs from the walk in another way. At the walk, the horse always has at least two feet on the ground, but this is not so at the trot. Starting with the left diagonal (near fore and off hind), the horse moves forward and the right diagonal pushes him off the ground in a sort of jump or bounce. We then have what is called "the moment of suspension" before the diagonal strikes the ground (*see* Fig. 78). During this moment of suspension, all four legs are off the ground. The moment of suspension is quite long in the racing Standardbred horse. He flies through the air for a long distance at each stride.

To start the trot, the commonly used leg cue is to squeeze with both legs at the same time. This tells the horse what gait is asked of him and so he does not confuse it with the leg cue for the walk which is the alternate squeezes of the leg.

A good trot is necessary as the horse learns to move forward freely, to extend his stride, and improve his balance. A long, free stride is necessary when the horse is ridden in circles (*see* Fig. 79). The horse who will trot freely is easier to train in his roll-backs. The extended trot does not cause problems with the jog-trot if the rider moves forward in the saddle, placing more weight on the stirrups while extending the trot. Then, as the rider sits down to jog, the horse soon learns what is expected of him.

The dictionary defines the lope as "to canter leisurely with a rather long, easy stride, as a horse." The canter and the lope have the same sequence of hoof beats. The English horse canters and the western horse lopes. The difference is that the canter is more collected than the lope. It is improper to ask the western horse to canter or the English horse to lope. (*See* Figs. 80 and 81.)

Fig. 76. In the trot, two legs move together—here the near hind and off fore. It is a two-time gait with the diagonal legs moving together.

Fig. 77. The off hind and near fore move together.

Fig. 78. Unlike the walk, the trot has a moment of suspension.

Fig. 79. The extended trot.

Fig. 80. The canter and lope have the same sequence of hoof beats. The canter, though, is an English gait that is more collected than the western lope.

Fig. 81. The lope is a three-time western gait. It is a long, leisurely stride.

The lope presents a new problem as the horse no longer travels straight, as he does at the walk and trot (*see* Fig. 82). All four-legged animals lope or gallop a little sideways, or on a diagonal. For an example other than a horse, watch a dog. A horse loping on the left lead would be loping with his forequarters a little to the right, his hindquarters a little to the left, and his head turned a little to the left. Consequently, the expression, the *lead*, comes from the fact that when on a left lead, the horse's left shoulder leads his right; his left hip leads his right; his left fore leads his right; and, his left hind leads his right (*see* Fig. 83). The green horse will lope on a more pronounced diagonal than the well-schooled horse who will lope nearly straight. At this gait, as elsewhere, a horse that travels straight is most desirable.

The lope is a three-time pace or gait. Assuming the horse to be on the right lead, the easiest way to understand the sequence of hoof beats is to start with the moment of suspension. At this time the horse is flying through the air with all four feet off the ground (*see* Fig. 84). The first foot to strike the ground will be the near hind (*see* Fig. 85) followed by the off hind and near fore together (*see* Fig. 86), and lastly, the near fore, or leading fore (*see* Fig. 87), as it is so often called. Then again, the horse floats through the air in suspension.

The moment the whole horse is suspended on the leading fore is the *time he vaults over the leading fore*. This is a critical moment; it is the time the flying change of leads can be made (*see* Fig. 88). Also, this is the time the rider squeezes with his legs to cause the horse's hind legs to shoot up under him in preparation for the stop on the hind legs. In the United States where races are run counter-clockwise, we find the racehorse running the curves on the left lead. Consequently, most bowed tendons occur, first, in the near fore. If we think of a thousand-pound horse running at speed and his entire weight dropping on one leg, this becomes easy to understand.

There is no general agreement as to the best way to obtain the desired lead. The majority of western trainers and riders, though, agree that the horse must be placed on the diagonal at which he will lope before he is asked to lope. What comes next is where the disagreement begins. For example, to get the left lead, some believe the proper procedure is to pull the horse's head to the right and with leg pressure, heels, or spurs signal him to lope from this position. The problem with this practice is that it causes the horse to lope with his head to the outside. This is incorrect.

The diagonal aids are used for many English-ridden horses. This means that to get the left lead, the left rein is used to flex the horse's

Fig. 82. Horses loping on a diagonal. In the lope, the horse no longer travels on a straight line.

Fig. 83. Horse loping on a diagonal.

Fig. 84. Suspension at the lope on a right lead. Since the animal does not run straight, the side which is ahead is referred to as the leading side. Figures 84 through 88 are a complete sequence of the lope.

Fig. 85. The horse comes down on the near hind.

Fig. 86. The off hind and the near fore come down together.

Fig. 87. Last down is the off fore or leading fore in this case. This is when the horse vaults over the leading fore into suspension, and is the moment when the rider can signal for a change of leads or best prepare for a stop.

Fig. 88. Here the horse has changed to a left lead. The off hind has come down first, having passed the near hind. The near fore passes the off fore and strikes the ground last.

head to the left and the rider's right leg is used to cause the horse's off hind to push him into the canter. This gives the proper head carriage and by using the opposite leg (the right leg for the left lead), the rider shoves the horse's quarters to a slight diagonal which helps to secure the correct lead.

The most generally used method for the western horse who neck-reins is to place him on the diagonal (again assuming the left lead is desired) by reining him to the right and at the same time placing pressure on his right side with the calf of the right leg. This causes the hindquarters to move slightly to the left, and also creates impulsion. Then, the rider reins the horse to the left in the line of direction in which he wishes to lope, and at the same time loosens the rein. The horse should then lope immediately without trotting. Any well-trained horse should go to the lope from the walk, and from the lope to the walk *without* trotting.

The horse can be taught to lope on the desired lead with a variety of cues. Some of these are the use of the outside leg only, the use of the inside leg only, and the use of both legs with the rein signaling which lead is desired. If we remember that in schooling the horse we are teaching him to give way to leg pressure, to move to the left, as in the sidepass, when pressure is applied with the rider's right leg, it then seems logical that the right leg should be used more strongly than the left for the left lead. This is the system used by most trainers. So, a rider who is mounted on a strange horse should have little difficulty in riding him.

My years in the horse business have convinced me that a standard set of cues helps to sell horses, as the buyer does not need to learn all the involved and intricate signals which some individual trainer has devised.

In addition to the slight diagonal required to get the lope, the rider must remember that the horse starts to lope at the moment his *leading hind* foot strikes the ground. At this time the horse can go from the walk to the lope *without* trotting.

The western horse has three gaits: walk, jog, and lope. To make it clear to him which gait is being asked for, a separate leg cue is used for each gait. The walk cue is alternate squeezes of the leg in time with the horse's hind leg. The jog cue is the squeeze of both legs at the same time. The lope cue is the squeeze with the calf of the rider's outside or opposite leg only. This procedure, especially in the show ring, has proven satisfactory, because the horse can understand what is asked of him.

The gallop, a gait similar to the canter or lope is different in that it is faster and is an extended gait, making it a gait or pace of four-time. Again, assuming the horse to be on the left lead, the first foot to strike the ground after the moment of suspension is the off hind, followed by the near hind, the off fore, and lastly the near fore. This sequence of hoof beats can easily be observed while a horse is running, for the strides are long and the horse floats through the air for a long distance.

In addition to the regular gaits—walk, trot, lope, canter, and gallop—we have the irregular ones: the amble, pace, single-foot, running-walk, fox-trot, slow-gait, and rack. None of these are desirable in the western horse which is being used in the show ring. However, the western horse who will be exhibited in horse shows must have only three gaits: the flat-footed walk, the trot, and the lope.

Chapter 8

Western Equitation

Equitation, horsemanship, and showmanship are the "Three Musketeers" of riding. None of these can be omitted from the successful rider's performance.

Nearly all trainers and riders hope to someday have that horse on which they can compete in horse shows with a reasonable expectation of bringing home a ribbon (*see* Fig. 89). Competition is keen in all of today's shows and neither the rider nor the horse can make mistakes and expect to win. To produce a winning combination there must be understanding between the horse and rider. One thought advanced by a novice horseman seems worthy of mention: "Don't try to show him who's boss, try to keep him from finding out."

The accomplished horseman knows that the show horse must be properly schooled. He realizes that the rider must know the rules of the class in which he is competing.

During the last twenty years I have conducted many classes and clinics, teaching adults and youngsters to ride. In these classes I have always used the AQHA and AQSA rule books as guides. At the start of each new class I ask for a show of hands from those who have even read the rule books and I am always amazed at how few hands are raised.

Knowledge of the rules of any sport is required of the participants and this surely applies to horse shows. Brigadier General Harry D. Chamberlin says in his excellent book, *Training Hunters, Jumpers, and Hacks:* "The horse show business is a game of specialists with special horses and is so considered in Europe." Of course, we in the United States believe our shows are equal to those of any other country and our horses capable of competing against all comers. We welcome competition and rivalry for they encourage the breeding of better horses and influence trainers to produce better-schooled horses and equestrians.

"Show business is show business and there is no business like show business," and this certainly applies to horse shows. Each exhibitor should realize that as long as he is in the ring he is closely watched and he must act accordingly. He must have his horse in show condition— clean; mane and tail brushed and free of tangles; the body coat bright and glossy; the long hair on jaws, nose, legs, and ears clipped; and the bridle path freshly roached. The horse should also be properly shod—a little hoof blacking will add to his appearance.

The rider's equipment should be clean and give the appearance of having been cared for. The rule book states that silver equipment may be used but shall not be given preference over good working equipment. There are many exhibitors who have expensive equipment, fine horses, and are attired in nice western clothes. They wear boots that are shined, and chaps and gloves that match their hat and costume. They even wear a tie! They carry a rope or reata, a pair of hobbles, and use a nice silver-mounted bit (*see* Figs. 90 and 91). These exhibitors are proud of their equipment and the appearance it creates. Though good working equipment is acceptable this does not mean that a dusty saddle, grass-stained bit, faded jeans, sweat-stained hat, and short-sleeved shirt, open at the neck are proper! (*See* Fig. 92.)

There are two well known and widely used sets of horse show rules: those of the American Quarter Horse Association and those of the American Horse Shows Association. Unfortunately, they don't agree on all things done in equitation classes or western classes, although the ultimate goal is quite similar. It seems a shame that a set of rules acceptable to both can't be agreed upon, but until they can, the exhibitor must learn both sets of rules. A copy of the rules of either association may be obtained by joining the association at a cost of ten dollars for adults and five dollars for juniors.

To many the word horsemanship means the same as equitation; there is a difference, though. The dictionary defines horsemanship as the art, skill, ability, or manner of a horseman, and equitation as the act of riding on horseback. Perhaps this is nit-picking but we find that the AQHA calls the class where the rider is judged the horsemanship class and the AHSA calls it the equitation class. The rules of both are very similar and the purpose of both is to improve the youngster's ways of riding and showing. There can be no doubt that horsemanship is necessary in an equitation class, but everything done in the class with the exception of dismounting and mounting is performed on horseback.

Before examining the rules of these classes we should remember there are many practices that have been accepted for years that don't show in the rule book. Whether a more detailed set of rules or a simpler one is needed is debatable. The pros and cons for each are many. There is no doubt that many of today's judges believe that the present rules are inadequate and that clarification is needed. However, whether you agree with the present rules or not you must follow them.

The AQHA rule book states riders will be judged on seat, hands, and ability to control and show the horse. Results shown by performance of the horse are *not* to be considered more important than the method used by the rider in obtaining them. Consideration shall be given to the size of the rider.

Appointments: This means the fittings and equipment of both the horse and rider. Clothing must be clean, workman-like, and neat. Tapaderos, spurs, and chaps are optional. Riders shall wear western hat and cowboy boots.

Tack: The saddle must fit the rider. It may be slick or swell forked, having a high or low cantle, but must definitely be sized to the rider. A half-breed, spade, snaffle, or curb bit may be used with split reins or romal. Mechanical hackamores, tie-downs, running martingales, and draw reins are prohibited. Hobbles and rope or reata are optional.

Class Routine: The judge will ask each rider to work individually. This work will be any of the maneuvers that the judge feels are necessary to determine the horsemanship ability of the rider.

The judge will use this individual work to determine the top riders whom he will call back for rail work.

Hands: Both hands and arms shall be held in a relaxed, easy manner with the upper arms *in a straight line with the body*. The hand holding the reins should be bent at the elbow. The free hand will be partially closed and held near the belt with the elbow bent causing the hand to be near, but not against the body, in front of that side. However, when using a romal the rider's off hand shall be around the romal with at least sixteen inches of it between the hands (*see* Figs. 93, 94, and 95). The hands are to be around the reins. One finger between the reins is permitted when using split reins but not with a romal. Reins are to be carried immediately above or slightly in front of the saddle horn. Only one hand is to be used for reining and that hand shall not be changed. Reins should be carried so as to have a *light contact with the horse's mouth*. At no time shall the reins be carried more than a slight hand movement from the horse's mouth. (*See* Figs. 96 and 97.)

Basic Position: The rider shall sit in the saddle with the legs hanging straight and slightly forward of the stirrups. (*see* Fig. 98). The stirrups should be just short enough to allow the *heels to be lower than the*

Fig. 89. Kathy Hale, winner of Youth Western Horsemanship receives her award.

Fig. 90. Silver inlaid bits and hobbles carried correctly.

Fig. 91. California-style closed reins, romal, and reata. The reata is carried incorrectly.

Fig. 92. Wrong! Short sleeved shirt and twisted body are not proper in any class.

Fig. 93. Good hand position. The ends of the split rein carried correctly in the off hand.

Fig. 94. When using split reins you can insert one finger between the reins; free ends mu be carried on side of the reining hand. This is not permitted with the romal.

Fig. 95. Good hand position. When using the romal there should be at least sixteen inches between the hands.

Fig. 96. The reins should be carried so that the rider always has light contact with the horse's mouth.

Fig. 97. This rider is holding the reins correctly in the California style.

Fig. 98. This shows correct posture according to the AQHA rules.

Fig. 99. The stirrups should be just short enough to allow the heels to be lower than the toes

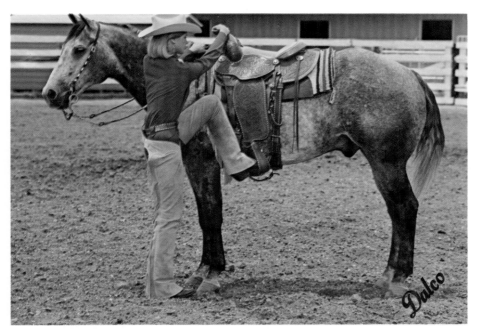

Fig. 100. This is the proper position for mounting from the shoulder.

Fig. 101. This is the proper position for mounting from the flank.

Fig. 102. It is incorrect to mount facing the side of the horse.

Fig. 103. The correct position for mounting with closed reins is: left hand above the horn with the romal on the off side.

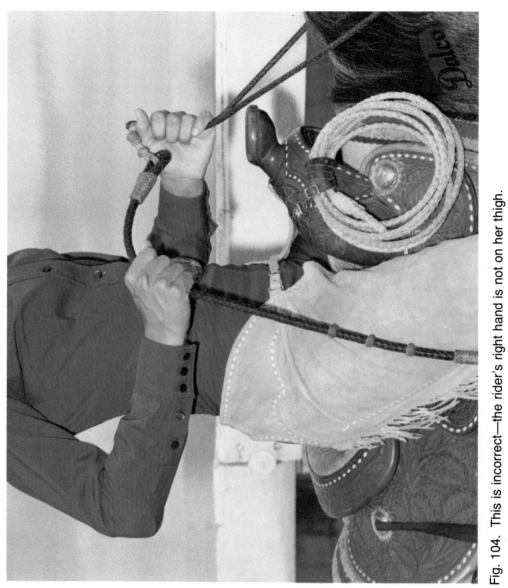

Fig. 104. This is incorrect—the rider's right hand is not on her thigh.

Fig. 105. This is the correct position—hands holding romal and closed rein with right hand on thigh.

Fig. 106. The rider, ready to dismount, is grasping the pommel and watching the horse's ears.

Fig. 107. This is the correct position after dismounting.

Fig. 108. The saddle must fit the rider. Hopefully, this rider will grow to fit his saddle.

Fig. 109. The feet should be placed flat on the tread of the stirrup.

Fig. 110. Riding pigeon-toed.

Fig. 111. Riding duck-toed or toed-out is a fault common to many young riders.

Fig. 112. Another problem common in young riders is riding with their feet in the corners of the stirrups.

Fig. 113. The correct position of the feet in stirrups is with the weight evenly distributed, the feet flat, and not too far home in the stirrups.

Fig. 114. This rider is leaning too far forward.

Fig. 115. This rider's feet are too far forward.

Fig. 116. This is the correct riding position. The rider's shoulders are perpendicular to the horse, her hand position is good, and her arm is in line with her body.

Fig. 117. This is a "twisted body position." The rider's arm is not parallel to her body and her hand is well in front of the horn.

Fig. 118. This person has an excellent mounted position with the hand correctly held above the horn.

Fig. 119. This young woman's hand is past the horn and her arm is not in line with her body. This is incorrect.

Fig. 120. This rider's feet are too far forward and the body is not straight up.

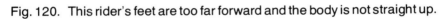

Fig. 121. This is the same rider as in Fig. 120 sitting correctly.

Fig. 122. The winner of the Horsemanship Class at Tucson, Arizona, demon-strates the California style of riding with closed reins. Her attractive color-coordinated outfit and excellent posture are sure to catch the judge's eye.

Fig. 123. Susan Kiekhefer riding Silk Stuff. This is what champions look like. These two held the 1974 AQHBA Senior Western Pleasure and Gelding titles and the 1975 AQHA Gelding and Champion Showmanship titles.

Fig. 124. Note the horse's "sour" ears.

Fig. 125. This horse's head is too low and the rider is holding the reins incorrectly.

Fig. 126. The left hand should be held above the horn.

Fig. 127. Well done. This rider has a nice costume and good carriage, though some judges might consider her heels too low.

Fig. 128. This case of "the bouncing bottom" is not incurable.

Fig. 129. The rider's posture is good, reins and romal are held correctly, but the reata is coiled incorrectly.

Fig. 130. Trisha Parker on Freckles Rocket. They were first in Western Horsemanship at the Lone Star End Show, 1975. Her left hand is not above the horn as required by the rules.

Fig. 131. Dwight Stewart instructing a class from horseback. Unlike some instructors he prefers this to teaching from the ground.

Fig. 132. A sliding stop done by ten-year-old Lisa Allen, showing excellent form.

Fig. 133. Carry Braman in a winning performance displays great control.

Fig. 134. Jana Jones on Fresno Smoky cutting in the Working Cow Horse Class.

toes. Feet may be placed home in the stirrups with boot heel touching the stirrup or may be placed less deep in the stirrup. Riding with *toes only in the stirrups will be penalized.* (*See* Fig. 99.)

Position in Motion: The rider should sit to the trot and *not post.* At the lope he should be close to the saddle. All movements of the horse should be governed by the use of imperceptible aids. Exaggerated shifting of the rider's weight is not desirable.

Riders are *not* required to dismount and mount under AQHA rules.

The rules of the AHSA state that riders will be judged on seat, hands, performance of horse, appointments of horse and rider, and suitability of horse to rider. A stock seat equitation class is a modified version of an open stock horse class.

Mounting and Dismounting: To mount, take up the reins in the left hand and place that hand on the horse's neck in front of the withers and with the romal or end of the reins on the near side. Grasp the stirrup with the right hand, place left foot in stirrup, then grasp horn with the right hand and mount (*see* Figs. 100, 101, and 102). If a romal is used it should be moved to the off side of the horse *after* mounting. The end of the split reins should remain on the same side as the hand holding the reins when the rider uses a finger between the reins. (*See* Figs. 103, 104, and 105.)

If the rider uses the right hand on the rein, the rope should be carried on the near side of the horse; the romal should remain on the near side at all times; and the end of the split reins should be moved to the off side.

To dismount, reverse the procedure and *step* down, looking toward the horse's ears. (*See* Figs. 106 and 107.)

In dismounting with split reins, it is optional whether the right rein is left up or taken down by the rider. Hands and arms shall be carried as shown in the AQHA rules.

Basic Position: Feet shall be placed in the stirrups with the weight on the ball of the foot. If stirrups are wide the foot may have the appearance of being home when in reality it is being properly carried on the ball of the foot.

Position in Motion: Again the same as in the AQHA rules.

Appointments: Clothing must be clean, workmanlike, and neat. Riders are to wear western hat, long sleeved shirt, and cowboy boots. Chaps *are* required unless management stipulates otherwise in the premium list. Spurs are optional. Judges *must* eliminate contestants who do not conform.

Tack: The saddle must fit the rider. Any standard western bit may be used unless management stipulates otherwise. Hackamores, tie-downs, running martingales, and draw reins are prohibited. If closed reins are used, hobbles must be carried attached below the cantle on the near side. Bosals or cavesson type nose bands are prohibited (*see* Fig. 108). A lariat or reata must be carried.

Class Routine: Horses are to enter the ring at a walk and be judged at a walk, jog, and lope both ways around the ring and be on the correct lead. Riders shall be able to perform not only the ring routine but also perform whatever additional tests the judge may ask of them. Horses shall be required to back in a straight line.

Correct riding can become a habit and I hope the photographs for this section will help you to ride correctly and win in the shows. We have now covered the rules in general with the exception of the rule governing curb chains. This states that they may be used, but must be at least one-half inch wide and lie flat against the horse's jaws.

Now, with the help of pictures, let's discuss the ways a rider can help his performance and offer a pleasing appearance to the judge. We will start with the feet and work up to the head. Each of the following pictures will help to show things *not* to do as well as the right way.

The feet should be placed *flat* on the tread of the stirrup (*see* Fig. 109). Riding pigeon-toed (*see* Fig. 110) or toed-out (duck-footed) (*see* Fig. 111), or in the corner of the stirrup (*see* Fig. 112) is incorrect by anyone's standards. The feet should be flat, not too far home, and the rider's weight evenly distributed (*see* Fig. 113). Those who want to ride with ox-bow stirrups and the foot home should have skipped this paragraph!

Most successful riders want their stirrups short enough for them to be able to stand in the stirrups at the walk, jog, or lope without having to lean forward or to pull on the reins or to grasp the saddle horn. When you get your stirrup position right, you'll find you are riding correctly. If your feet are too far ahead you can't do it. If they are too far back it won't work either. Remember that your toes can be turned out a little but never in!

A good way to find the correct length of your stirrups is to sit up straight in the saddle and look down over the point of your knees. If you can't see your toes, your feet are too far back and your stirrups are probably too short. If you can see your stirrups your feet are too far forward. A little variation at the lope is permissible because your leading foot will be ahead of the other.

When sitting correctly in the saddle, the rider should be in the middle, not leaning forward over the horn or back on the cantle, with the buttocks resting on it. He must sit on his crotch with his body erect, shoulders back, chest out, and head up (see Figs. 114, 115, and 116). Looking down at the ground just in front of the horse is *not* good. The rider's shoulders should be perpendicular to the horse, *not* with the hand that holds the reins ahead of the other, causing that shoulder to be ahead also. This is called twisted-body riding (*see* Fig. 117) and is very wrong.

Why? Because the rules state that the arms from the shoulder to the elbow must be in a straight line with the body (*see* Fig. 118), not extended forward (*see* Fig. 119).

Now we can understand why the hand must be held above the horn, for very few rider's arms are long enough to keep the upper arm in line with the body and the hand in front of the horn. In addition to twisting the body, the hand being in front of the horn causes the rider to begin to lean forward, spoiling his posture (*see* Fig. 120). Even this is not all of the harm done; as the rider leans forward he puts more weight on the stirrups and his feet go back. Lean forward in your saddle and watch where your feet go! Lean back and again watch what happens to your feet. I hope you understand, now, that the rules are justified and not for appearance only. (*See* Fig. 121.)

My observations as a judge lead me to believe that the rider presents a better picture if he rides with the ball of his foot on the stirrup. When doing this he can allow his heels to work up and down. He gets the benefit of the spring in his arch, ankle, knee, and even his hip. This not only makes for a smoother ride, it causes the horse to appear to have a smoother gait.

I have no objection to the feet being "home" when riding a colt, a cutting horse, or a reining horse, but in the show ring I believe it advantageous to ride on the ball of the foot.

"Sit up straight," "Ride proud," "Be tall in the saddle," are all wonderful expressions and each tells what is expected of the accomplished horseman. I believe the preceding pictures show some of the things *not* to do and how the wrong attire can detract from the overall picture. I agree with many judges who believe that the loose-fitting jacket and the suit coat, are not proper in a western class. (*See* Figs. 122 through 130.)

When explaining to youngsters the proper way to ride, I find that telling them that the man on horseback is a better soldier than the one on foot, helps them to understand. The man on horseback can go farther, travel faster, and carry more equipment than the foot soldier. The Great Wall of China was erected as a defense against the Mongolians who were mounted and with their horses were better fighters than the Chinese foot soldiers.

There are many expressions commonly used in horse shows and by instructors which every equestrian should know. One often heard is, "Take the rail to the right at the walk." Obviously, the rider isn't going to take the rail anywhere. He is being instructed to ride along the rail in the direction in which he can point his left hand toward the center of the ring.

Another direction often heard from the announcer is, "Come in and line up on the ring steward." This means that the judge has finished with the rail work and is ready to make his final inspection. The knowledgeable rider will jog right into line. Always come into it from the rear, never from the front. This way you won't have to turn around or back in.

Often, the judge will next ask the horses to back and they should, readily, and in a straight line. If the rider is asked to dismount and to remount, his horse should stand quietly while this is done; not walk off or turn sideways.

We have not covered all the mistakes a rider can make. For instance, "flying like a crow," is an expression used when the rider moves his elbows up and down instead of keeping them against his sides where they belong.

Unlike some instructors, I prefer to ride a horse that will perform anything that is being taught in that lesson when teaching a class. There seems to be less tension in the class and I can talk more freely while on horseback. The class and I get together and I use a four-step method. First I explain what the lesson is about. Then I ask them questions and when I get the right answers I show them on my horse (see Fig. 131). We work on the lesson until they can perform the task. Then I consider the lesson learned. During this time I change horses every hour. This enables me to get in a lot of schooling time on my own horses. Like all trainers, finding enough time for training is a problem for me.

When the class has finally lined up along the rail in some semblance of single file there are many admonitions to be given. These are simple rules every rider should remember. Keep your heels down. Sit up straight, with your shoulders back and your head up. Keep your reins even. Give your horse some slack, keeping a light contact with his mouth. In single file, don't get too close to the horse in front of you. Try to go at the same speed as the rest of the class. There are many more, but these will keep you out of some trouble.

After a particularly trying class, I sometimes think of the teacher who, after a day like mine, said, "If there is anything in reincarnation, I hope I return as a childhood disease!"

Figures 132, 133, and 134 show winning form in reining classes, medal classes, and equitation classes. These students kept the simple rules of my classes in mind. You try it, too!

Chapter 9

The Western Pleasure Horse

The western pleasure horse class may well be the most popular western class if exhibitor interest and participation are used as a measure. A class of forty horses is not unusual and when shows offer junior and senior classes as well as youth activities classes the number of entries mounts rapidly. Add to these, the classes found in open shows, such as owner to ride, amateur to ride, ladies, novice, lightweight, heavyweight, stallions, mares, geldings, and stake classes and the number of pleasure horses becomes astronomical.

The showing of the pleasure horse is more complex than a cursory examination reveals. Showmanship enters into this to a great degree, for the rider must try to make a favorable impression on the judge if he expects to win. Because of this aspect we see that a good rider can make a mediocre horse look good and a poor rider can make a good horse look bad.

The winner of the pleasure horse class often seems to float effortlessly around the ring. He makes no mistakes, such as wrong leads. He goes at the proper speed, and is riding a horse that is pleasing in appearance. Anyone watching such a performance must realize that he is seeing not only a well-trained horse, but an experienced rider as well. There is no record of a horse winning a pleasure class without a rider! (See Fig. 135.)

The rules of the pleasure horse class state that the horses are to be shown at the walk, jog-trot, and lope both ways in the ring, on a reasonably loose rein. The judge may request extended gaits and horses are required to back in a straight line. The American Quarter Horse Association rules state that the class will be judged on performance and conformation at the discretion of the judge. The American Horse Show Association rules spell it out by saying that the class is to be judged sixty percent on performance, thirty percent on conformation, and ten percent on appointments. The AQHA rules state that the rider shall wear western hat and cowboy boots. Spurs and chaps are optional.

The horse shall be shown with a stock saddle. Silver equipment will not count over good working equipment. A hackamore, curb, snaffle, half-breed, or spade bit is permissible. Chain curbs are permissible. A martingale or tie-down is prohibited. Use of a rope or reata is optional, but if used it must be coiled and attached to the saddle.

The AHSA rules differ in that the rider must wear western hat, cowboy boots, shotgun chaps or chinks, and carry a rope or reata. The same types of bits are acceptable, but the hackamore is not. All bosals and cavessons are prohibited. If split reins are used no hobbles are necessary, but if closed reins are used hobbles must be carried. (*See* Fig. 136.)

Not all Quarter Horse enthusiasts agree as to what is proper equipment for the horse. Some believe that any equipment will do, maintaining that the Quarter Horse shows are for rich and poor alike. Others believe that show business is show business, and both horse and rider will make a more pleasing impression if nicely appointed. My personal opinion is that anything that adds to the appearance of the horse and rider adds to their chances of winning a ribbon. As someone once said, "neat but not gaudy." (*See* Fig. 137.)

The part that conformation plays in the pleasure horse class must not be taken lightly. Some judges, though, attach less importance to this than others. If the judge doesn't like your horse there is very little possibility that he will use him.

Theoretically, the horse that wins the halter class should also win the pleasure class and in some instances this happens, but not often; many horses fitted for halter competition are not in working condition and are not trained for pleasure. So, before you load your horse and head for home after being excused from your halter class remember that not all those ribbon winners are suited for pleasure. Most top pleasure horses have a different way of going than that of reined horses! This statement is like opening a barrel of snakes; you don't know which one is going to bite you. The advocate of the all-around horse cries, "Not so!" The champion of the single-event horse says, "Bravo!" The question you must resolve is: Do you want a horse that wins a blue ribbon in one event or wins multi-colored ribbons in several?

The pleasure horse must give a smooth ride and to do this he must travel close to the ground. How a horse travels can be easily seen by viewing him from the side as he travels. The horse that has a high lift to his hips is usually better adapted to reining for he will learn to change leads easily. The horse with a low lift rides easier and makes the better pleasure horse.

Conformation has a direct bearing on how easy a horse's gaits are. The horse with the short neck, wide chest, straight shoulders, short pasterns, and straight forelegs doesn't ride smoothly. However, the horse with the Thoroughbred conformation isn't ideal either. He has too much spring to his gait and has a high lift to his lope. Conformation affects the way a horse moves his feet and legs and we find that they do many things at the trot that are not desirable. Undesirable characteristics are winging, forging, dragging the toes of the hind feet, and even limping. Some of these faults may be observed at the lope. Here, the high lift of the quarters is easily seen.

We sometimes hear someone criticizing the judge's decisions and this critic is basing his opinion on what he can see from his seat in the stands. It is highly improbable that he can see the horse's actions as well as the judge does. Any viewer of a class should keep in mind that he is seeing the performance from an entirely different angle than the judge. We see many judges who stand facing the side of the ring and watch each horse as it passes by. These judges can't see what takes place behind them while in many cases the audience can. The audience may sometimes see mistakes which escape the judge. But, while the onlookers are watching this horse and his problem, several horses are passing in front of the judge and he is evaluating the performance of each as well as the appearance of horse and rider.

Very few judges claim to be perfect and certainly no one can see everything that happens in a large pleasure class. This sounds like a defense of the judge, but after judging many shows over a long period of time, I know that it is easy to miss something that happens in the show ring.

We find another group of judges that prefers to stand in the corner of the ring. This group can see most of the arena at all times. However, this necessitates a lot of walking on the judge's part and is time-consuming from the management's point of view, time being a deciding factor in large shows. No matter where the experienced judge stands, he won't miss much of what takes place and he will go to the finals with good horses. An unknown wise man, who must have been to the same shows I have, said: "The judge whose opinion coincides with yours is obviously a rare gentleman, with good taste and perception."

Many horsemen believe that the color of the horse influences a judge's decision. This may be true; what horseman doesn't stop to look at a beautiful dappled gray, a gorgeous shining black, a golden palomino with flowing white mane and tail, or a lovely red sorrel? Beautiful horses, like beautiful girls, catch the eye, and to win you have to be seen and appreciated.

The rider's personal attire should be such that it adds to the overall picture of the horse, but it should not overshadow him. A rider could wear clothes that call attention to himself rather than to the horse. Faded jeans, sweat-stained hat, short-sleeved shirt, and no chaps may attract attention, though they don't present a favorable picture to the judge. (*Compare* Figs. 138 and 139 with Figs. 140 and 141.)

Time is precious at most shows and so the judge doesn't give much time to the walk. In less than one round the judge has ample time to observe the walk of each horse. Many judges prefer a good fast walk and will give a horse with such a walk preference over one that plods along. I wonder how many riders who had the choice between two horses to take for a pleasure ride would choose a slow walker over one that had a nice brisk walk. To emphasize this, the AHSA rules state that special emphasis shall be placed on the walk. This means a good, fast walk.

The height at which a horse carries his head can make a favorable or unfavorable impression on the judge. This varies with the section of the United States from which the judge comes. Those from the west coast prefer that the head be carried so the eyes are about the height of the withers or a little higher. They also want flexion at the poll or some finish, as they term it. To teach and to maintain this carriage there must be light contact with the horse's mouth through the reins and bit. There can be no collection (possibly this should be called semi-collection) on the loose rein. (*See* Fig. 142.)

Judges from the midwest prefer a low head carriage and flexion seems unimportant to them. The horse must go on a very loose rein. Sometimes it seems that the looser the rein the better the chance of winning. This has become a very controversial subject and possibly both sides need to give a little and meet somewhere in the middle. Until there is such a compromise, it is best to school the pleasure horse to perform either way and try to show him to please the judge officiating that day. (*See* Fig. 143.)

Proponents of each of these systems are firm in their beliefs. Many horsemen believe that the expression "on a reasonably loose rein," could be more properly called "light contact" (*see* Figs. 144-149). The loose, flopping rein, often seen in shows, loses all contact. Too much time is lost in gathering up the slack in order to control the horse, or to extend the arm full length to establish contact and control. With an extremely loose rein we find riders with the reining hand out beyond the horn. When this happens we see this rider with one shoulder far ahead of the other and the whole body twisted. The upper arm can no longer remain parallel with the body as required. (*Compare* Figs. 150 and 151 with Figs. 152 and 153.)

It is hard to understand why this method is popular in some sections of the country, because it isn't a comfortable position to maintain hour after hour. The rider with light contact need only flex his wrist and he has control of his horse, while the loose-reined rider must move his whole arm. Also, with a loose rein, the contact of the bit surprises the horse and up goes his head.

It has been said that horsemen hate change. This is probably the understatement of the year. It isn't easy to change a habit like the loose rein. It has been developed over many years in the saddle; besides, dad did it that way and so did granddad. (*See* Figs. 154 and 155.)

We have discussed the things a judge sees as a horse trots, some of which the onlooker can't see. Now, let's look at the lope. Again there are peculiarities that are difficult for the audience to see from their angle but that the judge can easily view. This gait also has its imperfections. One thing both the audience and the judge can see is how easy the horse appears to ride. Again, the horse with the high lift of his hips is not considered to be as nice a pleasure horse as one who travels along just above the ground in a smooth, easy fashion. As we saw in Chapter 7, the horse does not usually lope straight ahead, but on rather a slight or a decided diagonal depending on the horse. This is especially true of a young horse and most judges will not penalize a horse for the diagonal unless it is very acute. The finished horse, however, should travel straight, or nearly so. (*See* Fig. 156.)

As horse shows have become more popular and better-trained horses and riders compete, we find very few wrong leads and of course a horse detected on the wrong lead will be excused when the cut is made.

Faults the judge sees and counts against the horse are: the horse who resents another's passing him; who carries sour ears or switches his tail excessively; is passing the other horses continually; goes much slower than the rest of the class; fails to increase the speed of his gait when asked; fails to slow down upon request; becomes excited in a crowd; or doesn't stay on the rail where he belongs.

Winning a pleasure class hinges on rider technique as well as the horse. He must be ridden where he can be seen by the judge. The proper place is on the rail and not out in the center of the ring. Most judges resent being run over, spattered with mud, or covered with dust. The rider must endeavor to stay out of traffic which at times is not easy. Often the rider can gain a little distance from the horse ahead by riding a little deeper into the corner or by cutting the corner, depending on the problem confronting him. He may even make a small circle and return to the rail, without breaking gait, but this can't be done often and never in front of the judge.

It is not proper or even safe to pass between a horse and the rail if the horse that is being passed is within four feet of the rail. Not all riders know this and the accomplished showman will sometimes move to the inside to let a horse pass rather than have his horse distracted or made nervous by a horse that is too close behind him. The showman must be alert and try to maintain room to maneuver, keep an eye on the judge when possible without his being too obvious, watch the ring steward, and listen to the announcer. It is well to know your number; sometimes you only get called once.

Many things are accepted in horse show procedure that are not in the rule book—terms that have been used and accepted as proper. For instance, "Take the rail to the left," simply means ride along the rail going to your left, or if you are not sure of which way to go, ride so that your left hand is toward the center of the arena. We often hear the announcer command, "Walk your horses, come in, and line up." It is best to jog right into line and to enter from the rear, leaving room for the judge to walk around your horse. It is not proper to ride into line from the front and try to turn around in line, nor is it proper to try to back into line. It is much more polite and easier, too, to ride around the end of the line and then find a spot to line up. These things are just as improper as wearing your hat in the house, in church, or when dancing.

The rules state that horses must be worked both ways in the arena and at all three gaits. When this has been done the judge will often pick the horses he likes best, put them back on the rail, and excuse the rest. He can then select his winners from these finalists. It is mandatory that the horses being considered for placing be backed. Herein lies a trap, for although all horses should back readily, straight, and with the head in a normal position with mouth closed, it doesn't always come out that way! How embarrassing it is to have the horse everyone has picked as the winner refuse to back!

Both exhibitor and onlooker should remember that the placings of the judge are just his opinions and may or may not agree with theirs, and the next judge may change the placings of the same horses. This is just one man's opinion and should be accepted. Some judges prefer a low head carriage and the loose rein while some like more finish and light contact. When you have seen a judge tie one class you should be able to tell which he prefers and show your horse accordingly. (*See* Figs. 157 and 158.)

The controversy rages as to how to best train the pleasure horse. It centers around whether to train him in the arena or in the pasture. Before we try to decide which is better, let's take a brief look at the basic training every horse should have. Whether he was started with the longe line or the long reins and ground driving, he was first taught obedience and learned to have confidence in his trainer and in himself. Then he was ridden, first with the leading rein, then advancing to the open rein, and finally, the direct rein. He was taught to follow his head and to go forward freely.

His next lesson was the push-off or shoulder-in at which time he learned to give to leg pressure and finally to sidepass.

In his third lesson he learned to obey the bearing rein or neck rein. While being schooled in these exercises he became proficient at carrying his head at the correct height and responding to the leg cues as well as the oral commands. However, he still needed schooling in the desired speed at all gaits.

This training can be done in the arena or in the pasture. There are many pleasure horses, trained for show, who are trained in the arena and have no pasture riding for the simple reason that the trainer has no other place to ride. The danger in this procedure is the possibility of the horse becoming bored or "sour" from nothing but arena riding. (*See* Figs. 159, 160, and 161.)

The horse trained in the pasture or on the bridle trail has a different problem. He is not accustomed to arena work and the presence of other horses at his first shows causes him concern about the traffic and he doesn't perform at his best. The green horse needs lots of arena work and outside work too; the training of a pleasure horse is not done in just a few days. His performance must be nearly perfect if he is to win.

Before discussing the ways to train a young horse to go at the right speed at each gait, a short review of his gaits will indicate some of the problems that must be solved. The secret of training is a complete understanding of how his feet and legs move and how he must travel.

For instance, he must walk fast and travel straight. This is easier said than done, for few horses do this naturally. When watching a horse and rider approaching from a distance, if we see the horse walking rapidly, bobbing his head up and down, and coming as straight as an arrow, we should be immediately aware of two things: we are seeing a well-trained horse and an accomplished rider. (*See* Figs. 162 and 163.)

Chapter 7 describes the leg cues and if the horse was properly schooled, the walk should be reasonably well established. Again, it would be wise to remember that the horse must travel straight at the walk and the trot. The leg cue for the walk is alternate squeezes of the leg in time with the horse's hind leg. This makes him push a little harder and walk a little faster.

The jog-trot has also been taught in basic training, but now the horse must develop a jog that is easy to ride and learn to maintain a steady speed. Judges pay a lot of attention to the jog. If the horse appears hard to sit it will be difficult for him to place well in a large class. The standard leg cue for the jog-trot is a simultaneous squeeze with both legs.

The extended trot is expected in many shows and all pleasure horses should be able to extend and to return to the jog when requested. The rider can help the horse to extend by placing a little more of his weight on the stirrups and leaning forward while the horse is extended (*see* Fig. 164). Then, when he wants the horse to return to the jog, the rider sits down and the horse recognizes this as the cue to resume the jog.

Teaching the jog is easy if the rider will walk his horse until he is relaxed then jog for a short distance. If the horse is going a little too fast give a light pull on the reins (not a jerk) until the horse slows to the desired speed, then give him a little slack, or at least return to a light contact. If the horse speeds up again he is slowed again. In a short time he will maintain a constant speed.

The lope presents a more complex problem as the lead must be considered as well as the speed at which the pleasure horse should travel. Additionally, the horse will be judged on how readily he goes from the walk to the lope. There should be no trot steps in this change of gait. The horse will be judged on how smoothly he returns to the walk. Again, there should be no trot steps in this change.

At the time the green pleasure horse is asked to lope, a slight tightening of the reins and a little diagonal is permissible. With the finished horse there should be only an imperceptible cue and very little diagonal as he starts to lope.

Many pleasure horses will immediately take the right lead from a squeeze of the rider's left leg or the left lead from a squeeze of the right leg. The part of this action that is particularly important is the movement of the horse's hindquarters to the right at the squeeze of the rider's left leg which puts the horse on the diagonal from which he can take the right lead. The diagonal takes its name from the front leg involved.

On a right diagonal this action causes the right hind leg to move up under the horse so that he is in position to lope. He can go from the walk to the lope without trotting just as his leading hind foot strikes the ground, and he *departs*—he starts to lope without trotting. At any other time in his stride he must either trot or walk until this point is reached and then lope. One step later he must go through the complete cycle or he may start on the wrong lead.

If the western rider was riding with a rein in each hand, as would be done with a horse ridden with English equipment, he could teach the horse to select the correct lead by signaling with the rein. Thus, a light touch of the left rein would indicate the left lead. This can't be done by the rider of the western horse because he is holding both reins in one hand. However, he can accomplish somewhat the same result by reining his horse to the direction opposite the desired lead and then loping as he reins in the direction he wishes to go. This works well with green horses and green riders providing the horse is not allowed to lope as he is reined in the opposite direction for then he is put on the counter-lead or the wrong lead. When working in an arena this simply means that the rider reins his horse toward the fence and lopes as he comes away from it.

The wrong lead is the cardinal sin in a pleasure horse class. The transition from walk to lope is easy for the horse who has been taught collection. Possibly this should be called semi-collection, for most western horses are not truly collected as is the dressage horse. The advanced rider can tell by feel whether his horse is in position to select the correct lead before he departs and will not let him lope until he is in the proper position.

The left leg for the right lead and right leg for left lead is a standard method employed by most successful trainers. We find a few, though, who use the left leg for the left lead which is contrary to the teachings of equitation as the horse is being schooled to *give* to leg pressure. This causes problems when the horse is taught the flying change of leads. Additionally, most riders have been taught the standard method and

Fig. 135. Mrs. Ruth Stewart on Dandy Moolah.

Fig. 136. If closed reins are used, you must carry hobbles.

Fig. 137. Correct attire and appointments, California-style. The rider's attire should add to the overall picture of the horse but not overshadow it.

Fig. 138. Faded jeans and no chaps do not present a favorable picture to the judges.

Fig. 139. Many judges do not consider short sleeves and coat proper attire for the Western Pleasure Horse Class.

Fig. 140. Susan Simmons and Robin Jag display the style that has made them champions. A pretty girl, a nice horse, proper attire and appointments, and excellent posture will always score well.

Fig. 141. Linda Anderson riding well and nicely attired. Her posture is erect and her hands and reins are held correctly. When the rider is right, the horse will be too.

Fig. 142. Collection on the rail, head held high with flexion at the poll; this is the west coast look.

Fig. 143. The woman is holding with light contact.

Fig. 144. Many midwest judges prefer a loose rein and low head carriage. The loose rein is sometimes called the Texas-style rein.

Fig. 145. This is an example of light contact and good head carriage.

Fig. 146. This pleasure horse carries its head too low when ridden with a loose rein.

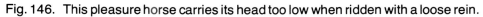

Fig. 147. When ridden with light contact, the same horse shows a better appearance and carriage.

Fig. 148. A pleasure at the lope with no contact. Note the poor head carriage.

Fig. 149. The same horse as in Fig. 148 ridden with light contact. Note the improvement in head carriage.

Fig. 150. This demonstrates poor posture. The rider has twisted her body. The horse has a low head carriage.

Fig. 151. To keep a loose rein this rider has twisted his body. The horse has "sour" ears.

Fig. 152. Here is a good example of low head carriage, maintained by light contact. The rider has good posture with the hand held correctly above the horn.

Fig. 153. Tee Jay Silver is well-ridden. The rider is maintaining good low head carriage with light contact. His hand is above the horn and his overall posture is good.

Fig. 154. This man is in *competition* looking like this! You must always remember that this is *show* business. Also, a rein as loose as this must startle the horse when contact is established.

Fig. 155. Billy Goen, a well-known Dallas trainer, riding with light contact.

Fig. 156. Dave Page in the Lone Star Show, 1975, shows his horse loping with the head carriage preferred in the midwest.

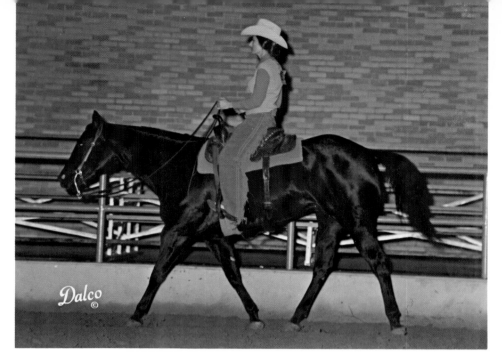

Fig. 157. Cookie Moreland shows the right way to ride at the jog. She rides with light contact, split reins held above the horn, good posture, and appropriate attire—a good showman.

Fig. 158. At the jog this horse looks good despite the rider's faults. The rider is holding the reins poorly and sitting back on the cantle.

Fig. 159. Harry Stickler on Miss Blue Moolah training in the pasture.

Fig. 160. John Ness on Dandy Moolah training in the arena. Both ways—the pasture and the arena—work well.

173

Fig. 161. Linda Anderson on an arena-trained horse, moving nicely.

Fig. 162. This horse is walking fast, but not travelling straight.

Fig. 163. This horse is walking fast and straight. It takes a well-trained horse and an accomplished rider to achieve this.

Fig. 164. An extended trot. (Mrs. Ruth Stewart.)

Fig. 165. Lanham Riley on Lightning Rey, a Stewart-trained horse. Lightning Rey is a Supreme Champion and has been shown in the Reining, Working Cow Horse, Western Riding, Pleasure Horse, Trail Horse, and Roping Classes.

175

Fig. 166. Holly New Year, winner of the Junior Horse Futurity, 1975, ridden by Don Parker.

Fig. 167. Hobby Knox, 1975 World's Champion Western Junior Riding Horse, Honor Roll Western Riding Stallion, and Superior Western Pleasure Horse ridden by Mehl Lawson.

can easily ride most horses without involved instruction as to the intricate cues some trainer has conceived.

There is one more cue that helps the pleasure horse perform more smoothly and that is the one used at the time he comes from the lope to the walk, without trotting. It is quite simple: The rider leans back just a little and takes the reins with him. This produces a little different action from just pulling on the reins to slow down. The horse soon recognizes this signal and comes to the walk smoothly without opening his mouth or throwing his head. Horses pay particular attention to the rider's weight and balance and they respond quickly to this change of the rider's position in the saddle.

The trainer continually tries to improve his horse and as he improves he becomes a pleasure to ride. It's easy to imagine a person going for a ride in the park, or down the trail, or just a ride to relax after dinner. If this person had the choice of several horses he would in all probability pick one with a good fast walk, a smooth easy jog, a nice lope, and one that was attractive in appearance—a pleasure to ride.

This would also apply to the cowboy. If his horses were equal at cow work he would probably prefer the one with the easy gaits (*see* Fig. 165). No one likes a horse that pokes along at the walk, trots with his hind feet kicking up a cloud of dust, and lopes on one lead only.

Most horses have to be taught to walk fast and to travel straight and the method of walking with your horse (alternate squeezes of the rider's legs) will produce a fast walk on most horses. This walk can be taught in the arena, but it seems easier to teach it outside in the pasture, or on the bridle trail (especially when headed for home). To teach this the rider must stay alert and really work at it. It requires a lot of patience.

Fortunately, the trot is a natural gait and doesn't have to be taught, but the jog-trot and the extended trot require a lot of schooling. Some riders believe the extended trot hinders the teaching of a good jog but this is not a majority opinion. The horse who moves freely has better balance and doesn't develop the lazy jog, dragging his hind feet.

The arena is a fine place for teaching the trot and circles are of great benefit in basic and advanced training. On the circle, the horse learns to go forward freely and improves his balance. He also learns to accept his bridle, to flex both laterally and vertically, and to go at the required speed. The rider must sit the trot in all western classes, but there is nothing wrong with posting the trot while training. Many western riders do, but not at the jog-trot.

The rider can aid the horse in the extended trot by placing more weight on the stirrups and by leaning forward, which becomes a cue to the horse to trot fast. The reins should be slack at this time, then, as the rider sits down in the saddle and takes a light contact with the horse's mouth, this becomes his cue to jog. If he is jogging a little faster than he should, a steady strain on the reins will slow him to the desired speed. Then the reins should be released until there is only a light contact with his mouth. If he speeds up, repeat this process over and over until he goes at the proper speed. There must be no jerks or tremors in the reins. These may help to teach flexion but are not good for teaching proper speed.

The young horse can also be taught to lope slowly in the arena. Again it must be said that many show horses never have a chance to be ridden outside. However, if pasture or trail riding is available it will certainly aid in this schooling. Circles, circles, circles—do many circles at the lope. Rather than slow the horse too much by pulling on the reins, just keep on going around and he will slow down of his own accord. Whether he reasons that he is not going anywhere is debatable but nevertheless he will slow down. When he lopes slowly in circles he can be taken to the rail and if he speeds up, he can be ridden into a circle until he slows and then taken back to the rail.

There can be no question of the value of riding the horse outside of the arena. Many believe that the modern riding horse should receive most of his early training outside the arena.

The companionship of man, his horse, and his dog are age-old and the thrill of a gallop through the countryside is still enjoyable to all. There is no reason to restrain the young horse from a gallop when he is fresh, if he can be controlled. After he has the play out of him is the best time to start his schooling.

There is no difficulty in teaching the horse to lope well enough for outside riding; this is only a matter of slowing the gallop until the three-beat lope is established. However, this is not good enough for the show ring. He must lope more slowly, and with some degree of collection, if he is to be shown on the west coast. Some collection creates a more impressive picture trainers and showmen from that area believe. The midwest attaches less importance to this and many classes are won by horses who have no collection. Although this has been mentioned before, it seems a good idea to stress this since judges from different parts of the country differ in their opinions and it is wise to show the horse in the manner the judge prefers.

Schooling the horse in the open can be started as soon as he relaxes and will walk quietly. He should be started at the lope with as little rein pressure as possible and allowed to lope at his regular speed. This will be too fast for the arena or show. He should have practice on both leads. If he doesn't take one as readily as the other he should be started on it more often until he is equally proficient at both.

Pulling on the reins to slow the horse is not a good procedure. It is best to let him lope a hundred yards or so even though he is going too fast. Then he should be brought to the walk by the rider leaning back and taking as little pressure on the reins as possible. The use of the voice will aid this and even if it takes several strides for him to come to the walk he will soon learn that this is the cue to come to the walk. He will pick this up much faster than you expect. He can be allowed to walk for fifty yards or so. While he is walking, a pat on the neck and some kind words will encourage him and add to his confidence. This procedure can be repeated for twenty or thirty minutes each day and in two or three weeks he will understand that he is to lope a short distance slowly.

There remains one more action the pleasure horse must perform in the show. It is mandatory that the judge ask those being considered for a ribbon to back. The horse should back readily, straight, and with his head in a normal position and his mouth closed. Knowlegeable trainers believe that all well-trained horses should do this and to accomplish it, patience in training is necessary. As the horse is being taught to back, a step or two at a time is enough; then a few more steps as the days go by until he will back twelve or fifteen feet in a straight line. Again, impulsion must play an important role for just as the horse is ridden forward, so must he be ridden backward.

Although every colt or horse can step back if he wants to it is not a natural thing and he will try in every way to turn before he will back. He cannot back the same way as he walks—each foot moving individually. Instead he must back by moving the diagonal legs together as he does at the trot.

Teaching the horse to back is best started on the ground. The trainer stands in front of the horse and tells him to back, at the same time stepping toward him and administering some light taps against his chest with the whip. Usually the horse will obey.

One or two steps is enough and there should be no pressure on the bridle while this is being done. When he backs readily on the ground the same procedure may be used from a mounted position. Again only a step or two at first. Then try with very light pressure on the bridle until he backs easily. He is being taught that backing is really a forward movement but he is going in the opposite direction.

To aid him in backing, impulsion (forward motion) helps in this way: The rider squeezes with his legs as though he intends to ride forward. Just as the horse's body starts ahead, but before he takes a step, light pressure of the reins resists the forward motion and, as the rider continues his leg pressure, the horse steps back. He backs until the rider's legs and hands release.

These principles will produce a pleasure horse that is comfortable to ride and pleasing in his appearance. The principal factors which must be considered are those which influence the judge's decisions: performance, conformation, and horsemanship. The judge's personal preferences as to how high or low the head is carried, how much collection is desired, and what speed he thinks the horse should show in the arena are important, but he is only trying to find the horse that looks and acts like it would be a pleasure to ride. (*See* Figs. 166 and 167.)

Chapter 10
The Trail Horse

It would be possible to write a book about trail horses by drawing on articles written by Mac McHugh, a noted trainer in Diamond Bar, California. I have done just this, for he has covered the subject so completely that no one can avoid doing so. (*See* Figs. 168 and 169.)

Perhaps you think of the trail horse as one not good enough for the pleasure horse class. Not so! In addition to working the rail, as does the pleasure horse, he must negotiate many natural and unnatural obstacles. In doing this, rider's errors are numerous. A nervous rider can cause a horse to make a mistake. To avoid some of these rider's errors it is necessary for the rider to know the rules of the class.

Fortunately, they are the same as those of the pleasure horse class regarding the rail work, appointments of the horse and rider, and the way the reins may be handled. (*See* Figs. 170 and 171.)

The AQHA rules state that six obstacles will be used; three of which are mandatory. They are: opening, passing through, and closing a gate; riding over at least four logs; and riding over a wooden bridge. Optional obstacles are: water hazard; hobble or ground tie horse; carrying an object from one part of the arena to another; backing horse through an L-shaped course; putting on and removing slicker; dismounting and leading horse over obstacles not less than fourteen inches high and not more than twenty-four inches high; and sending horse freely into trailer. (This last obstacle is not allowed in youth activity classes.) (*See* Fig. 172.)

The AHSA rules are very similar. They ask that the handle of the gate be at least forty-eight inches high. They stipulate that the rider must open and close the gate without losing control of it. The rider may be asked to dismount and remount from the off side. The sentence that really opens the bag of tricks is: *He shall perform over natural conditions encountered along the trail!*

What a trail ride some of the show managers must have taken! Whether it was on a safari into Kenya or a camel trip into Tibet, it

Fig. 168. Mac McHugh on Seatac, two-time AHSA Western Pleasure Horse of the year.

Fig. 169. Maggi McHugh on Abril, winner of the Open Trail Horse Stake at Del Mar, 1971.

Fig. 170. Becaco Badger #37, a fine pleasure and trail horse, was second in the Western Pleasure Class at the Cowtown Posse Show, 1974, ridden by Patty Swett.

Fig. 171. Silkworm, the 1975 "A" Champion Pleasure Horse, Pacific Coast, and the 1975 World Champion Junior Trail Horse at Louisville, Kentucky.

Fig. 172. Cynthia Cantleberry and Katy O'Grady have been the Pacific Coast Champions for four years in the Trail Horse Class. Here they show what made them winners at every "A" show on the Pacific Coast.

certainly had to be exciting! Can you imagine your trail horse quietly and peacefully passing his natural enemies such as lions, tigers, bears, or other predators? Even if they are in a cage or securely fastened they are bound to cause a horse some concern. Strange as it may seem, these animals have been used to increase the difficulty of negotiating the course.

Some exhibitors have indicated a reluctance to enter classes of this kind and so we find this practice generally discontinued. However, it is not unusual to find a goat, sheep, hog, or burro tied to the bridge you must cross or to discover a crate of chickens, ducks, geese, or guinea fowl along the course.

Not everyone has access to these animals while training his trail horse. Even without these added hazards we find that not all horses are suitable for the trail horse class. There are horses who will quietly cross a large black log and refuse to cross a small light-colored one. Disposition is paramount. The nervous horse, the one inclined to shy, and the young horse are not suitable for this event.

Judges do not like a horse who approaches an obstacle and rushes over it or may even seem to be looking at the grandstand while performing. We might think of how riding this horse on an unknown trail on a dark night might cause the rider some uneasiness! Knowledgeable judges and trainers believe that a horse should approach an obstacle with caution. They believe that his head should be lowered so that he can see clearly. He should have complete confidence in his rider and proceed when urged without repeated refusals. (*See* Figs. 173 and 174.)

Most horses resent going into water until they are accustomed to it and this is especially true of muddy water for they are unable to see how deep it is. They can be schooled to water hazards by first riding them through shallow water and gradually through deeper water until they will trust the rider and go where directed.

Riding horses over bridges and logs can be taught in the same manner by starting with low, or small ones and gradually increasing the height. Often a horse will refuse to cross a bridge or some obstacle on the ground, such as a tarp, white plastic, or cowhide. In schooling him to these obstacles it is much easier to lead him over them a few times than to try to ride him over them. After he has been led across the objects he fears, he will cross them while mounted. (*See* Fig. 175.)

We must remember that in training the trail horse much patience is needed. Any punishment inflicted to get the horse to approach or cross an object he fears is often associated with the object and he becomes more fearful of it.

Teaching the horse to ride over logs is easy if the rider starts with one log. When the horse negotiates it easily another log may be added and then another until he quietly crosses eight or ten logs. They may then be moved closer together and the distances between them staggered. Logs ten or twelve inches high are best for training. (*See* Figs. 176 and 177.)

At first the horse seems awkward or clumsy as he crosses a series of logs, but practice will soon improve his performance. He should not be whipped or spurred for stepping on a log; as he learns to place his feet between them he will stop this. If the logs are placed close together he should approach them slowly, but if they are a stride apart a brisk walk is better.

The trail horse must allow his rider to carry any conceivable items while on him. A favorite at shows is a bucket of rocks. The sight of the bucket and the accompanying noise of the rocks often distracts a horse and so some schooling is needed to get the horse to allow his rider to

Fig. 173. Katy O'Grady has won *every* "A" stake at one time or another.

Fig. 174. Lynn Rubel and Carmel Jack went to the National Finals three years in a row. A pretty girl on a pretty horse is always tough competition.

Fig. 175. Kathy Hale leading a mare over the logs in training.

Fig. 176. Twelve-year-old Tina Vail, on Princess Anna, winning the Trail Horse Class.

188

Fig. 177. When crossing logs, the horse should be allowed to keep its head down to see at close range.

carry noisy objects while on his back. There are some shows which furnish a dummy about the size of a human. This must be carried either in front of the rider or behind him. If your horse won't ride double this can cause a problem.

A common article encountered in the trail horse class is the slicker or raincoat which the rider is required to put on and remove while his horse stands quietly. The horse who will allow this with the reins looped around the horn earns a better mark. Home training can easily accustom the horse to this.

Another favorite object of show managers is a log which the horse is required to drag. A sack of cans is sometimes substituted for the log and the noise of this sack of cans may alarm a green horse. (*See* Figs. 178 and 179.)

Many trail horse classes include a ground tie as one of the obstacles. The rider is asked to dismount and leave his horse (perhaps to walk to a mailbox) and return while the horse remains standing where he was left. When split reins are used they are just dropped to the ground and the horse, theoretically, remains tied to the ground until his rider returns. (*See* Fig. 180.)

Fig. 178. The trail horse must allow his rider to carry any conceivable item while on him. Here the rider carries a bucket of cans.

Fig. 179. Competitors in the Trail Horse Class must be ready for anything. Here, a horse and rider drag a log. This is a favorite of show managers.

Fig. 180. R.O. Yesterday is ground-tied by split reins.

When closed reins are used the AHSA rules stipulate that hobbles must be carried and may be placed around the horse's legs while his rider leaves him. This should all be accomplished in a friendly way. (*See* Fig. 181.)

Horses are required to back through many kinds of obstacles of various widths and lengths. They are asked to back through L-shaped courses. These are sometimes mounted on buckets or some other object which will allow the rails to fall if bumped. Practice for this is time consuming but necessary, because nearly all shows have some type of backing course. (*See* Fig. 182.)

Teaching the horse to back through obstacles is easy if the rider starts with just two poles spaced wide enough for the horse to go through easily. Don't be surprised if on the first attempt the horse doesn't back between the poles as you had expected, and don't kid yourself that he can't see them and is accidentally missing them.

It is best to ride in between the poles until the horse is part of the way out of them and then back through them. He should back slowly. This must be repeated several times and each time he should be ridden a little farther out of them before backing.

Fig. 181. R.O. Yesterday is ground-tied with closed reins and hobbles.

Fig. 182. Horses are required to back through many kinds of obstacles in the Trail Horse Class. Backing through the "L" while looking to the inside of the turn is the correct way.

Fig. 183. This is incorrect. The horse should be parallel to the gate.

Fig. 184. The rider must be able to reach the gate latch and open and control the gate. This is the correct position for the horse and rider.

You still have a surprise coming! By this time your horse will back straight and true between the poles and so you now ride him to the end of the poles, turn him around, and back through them (or do you?). To the horse this is a whole new ball of wax. You are using the same poles, in the same place, spaced the same distance apart, but you are approaching them from a different direction. His posterior vision is functioning in high gear and after all, this wasn't his idea to begin with. Usually some patience and kindly persuasion will prevail.

Negotiating the L-back-through presents another problem. The horse must turn his haunches at pressure from the rider's leg as he makes the right angle turn. The rider can help him by looking to the inside of the turn. As the horse's hind feet get to the turn the rider must squeeze with his leg to start the horse's hindquarters in the new direction and rein the fore hand to the opposite direction. This turn should be negotiated very slowly.

One of the mandatory obstacles in trail horse classes is the gate. Opening and closing a gate while on horseback is not difficult. If the horse has been taught the sidepass, he will sidle up to it as he should. When the horse will only turn his head to the gate it becomes nearly impossible for the rider to open and close it without losing control of it, as demanded by the rules. (*See* Fig. 183.)

The horse should approach the gate so that his hindquarters are at the hinge end of the gate. He should be parallel with it and close enough for the rider to reach it with ease. (*See* Fig. 184.)

Unless instructed otherwise by the judge, the rider should open the gate and push it away from him (*see* Figs. 185 and 186). The horse should be backed a step or two until his nose clears the gate post and ridden through the opening and around the end of the gate.

As the horse passes through the gate he should not leave a wide opening through which an animal might escape. (*See* Fig. 187.) He should be kept across the opening while the gate is being closed (*see* Fig. 188). Backing the horse a step or two, as soon as his hindquarters clear the gateway, helps to keep this opening covered and also aids in closing the gate.

Every horse should load into a trailer and, as there have been many articles written on how to teach a horse to load, I have omitted this from this chapter. However, it must be remembered that this obstacle is encountered in many shows although it is prohibited in Youth Activity classes.

Jumping or leading over a jump that is not less than fourteen inches high and not more than twenty-four inches high is commonly encoun-

Fig. 185. Once the latch is undone, push the gate open.

Fig. 186. Trisha Parker on Freckles Rocket demonstrates the correct way to open the gate on her way to a third place finish in Western Riding at the New Mexico State Fair, 1975.

Fig. 187. This is the wrong way to open the gate—the horse should be across the opening to prevent the stock from escaping.

Fig. 188. When done properly, the horse blocks the gate opening while the gate is being closed.

Fig. 189. Chris Underwood leading her horse over a jump.

Fig. 190. When jumping in western saddle watch for the saddle horn; it has a way of intruding on the abdomen of the unwary.

tered and all horses should do this with ease. The horse who was schooled on the longe and longed over Cavaletti (a series of poles or logs laid on the ground) will have no difficulty with this obstacle. (*See* Fig. 189.)

Any horse can negotiate a two foot jump, but jumping in a western saddle can become dangerous unless the rider is accomplished, because the saddle horn has a way of intruding on the abdomen. However, a low jump should present no great problem to an accomplished rider. (*See* Fig. 190.)

Training the trail horse requires a lot of time and patience and like all show horses he should have a reasonable amount of collection. He must go forward freely with his head in the correct position. He must accept his bridle and relax his lower jaw. He must be under control through the reins and by pressure of the rider's legs. He must have complete confidence in his rider and go wherever his rider directs him. His head must be free in order to lower it at obstacles to inspect them. He must be a special horse!

Chapter 11

The Reined Horse

"The horse is God's gift to man," says an old Arabian proverb. No true horseman will refute this statement. Though, it should be said that the horse is of little value without a man to ride him.

When we speak of the reined horse, or what's called the stock horse on the west coast, we are talking about that exceptional horse who has the will and the athletic ability to rise above the ordinary horse. He has the courage and willingness to extend himself to the utmost. Even so, without an excellent trainer and rider, this horse can never reach the peak of performance required to win the big shows.

Reined horsemen are proud of their horses and have even been known to brag a little on their horse's performance. When they gather together, expressions such as: "thirty-foot slide," "the ground roared under him," "he spun like a top," "light as a feather," "buried his tail in the ground," and many others are common. (*See* Figs. 191 and 192.)

We must remember that there are two distinct methods of riding and training horses in the United States. On the east coast they teach the use of the flat saddle, full bridle, and two reins (actually there are four reins). This system is virtually unchanged since the Romans taught it to the Anglo-Saxons who brought it to America before the States were united. This system still has a place in the horse world of today. Seldom, though, do we find a reined horse schooled in this manner. This is not an attempt to discredit this system. I only wish to point out that most reined horses are schooled in a different way. (*See* Fig. 193.)

The ways and equipment of the western rider are completely different. They are adapted to the work done with horses and cattle. The great ranches of the west needed riders and horses to perform the work that couldn't be done by riders of the flat saddle. Even the western equipment has changed through the years, so that today we find both California and Texas styles in vogue, each with its differences in equipment. (*See* Figs. 194, 195, and 196.)

Fig. 191. Tom Gilmore stopping Aries Star.

Fig. 192. Ed Cridge on his Hi-point reining horse.

Fig. 193. The full bridle is often called the double bridle. It is used in training with the flat saddle.

Fig. 194. This California-style silver bit, rein chains, and closed reins is a beautiful piece of work.

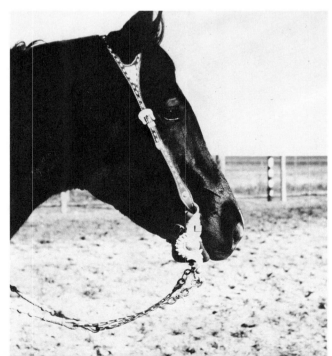

A brief look at history shows us how the English and western styles came into being. As we trace them down through the years we see why even the western system divided.

The history of the horse and his earliest use gives us an insight into how he was first used and how he progressed through the centuries to the horse of contemporary times. Whether knowledge of how the horse was domesticated helps in training is debatable, but among educated horsemen there is a curiosity that goes beyond the need of its immediate use. They are interested in what the horse was first used for and how he progressed to his present degree of usefulness.

History doesn't tell exactly why, when, or how man first domesticated the horse, but we believe it was later than 4000 B.C. It is believed that it was done on the great Steppes north of the mountain ranges, bordering on the Black Sea and the Caspian Sea. This was done by a people who spoke an Indo-European (Aryan) language.

These people kept no written records, but the people south of the mountain ranges did. They knew of the horses in the mountains. Records of the horse have been found on clay tablets of the era 3000–2000 B.C. By about 1800 B.C., horses were mentioned in connection with chariots. Between 1750 and 1700 B.C. the Aryans migrated to Mesopotamia and brought many horses with them. The greatest weapon of war of that time was the horse-drawn chariot.

Riding may have come before driving. The first pictures of men riding horses come from the tomb of Horenhab in fourteenth-century B.C. Egypt. These men were riding bareback! Around 747-727 B.C. Assyrian warriors were riding with saddle cloths secured by a breastplate and a crupper.

These horsemen were using a bit that was a simple bar with a rein attached to each side. The rider pulled on one rein or the other to turn the horse and rode with a rein in each hand (see Fig. 197.) This bit was later replaced with one that had a joint in the middle. This was the start of the snaffle bit. This is a mild bit; to make it more severe, the Greeks and Romans of the sixth century used a bit with sharp spikes on the mouthpiece. Some of these bits were fitted with a short piece of chain dangling from the mouthpiece and some had rollers for the horse to play with. The rollers, or crickets, in our modern bits are very similar to these. We still have snaffle bits with similar devices for horses to play with. It is believed that these devices help to keep the horse's mouth moist. (See Fig. 198.)

The origin and the originator of the bit are unknown. It seems probable that both bit and stirrup (the first saddles had no stirrups)

Fig. 195. Harry Stickler of Watsonville, California, shows appointments and attire typical of west coast shows.

Fig. 196. Trisha Parker and Freckles Rocket were first in horsemanship and third in reining at the New Mexico State Fair, 1975. The appointments and attire shown here are those favored in the midwest.

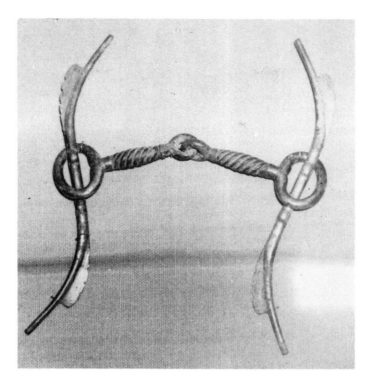

Fig. 197. This is a Chinese bit from the Han Dynasty (25 A.D.–220 A.D.). The saddle and stirrup probably originated in China, also. They were brought to Europe in the sixth century by Atilla.

Fig. 198. Spoon spade with copper braces and cricket (roller).

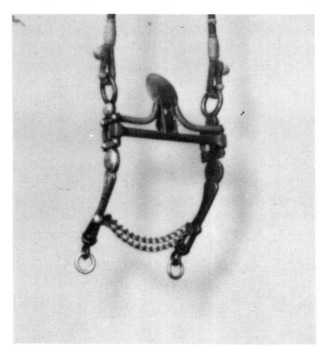

originated in China. The saddle was brought to Europe in the sixth century by the most fearsome barbarians of them all: the Huns.

About 400 B.C., Xenophon wrote *The Art of Horsemanship*. It was the first book written on equitation. In it he states that at that time most men rode naked! Xenophon's work is still important. It has been said that, "encountering a quotation from him is like meeting an old friend." Many of his ideas are still considered basic in today's training practices despite them being more than 2400 years old.

Xenophon said: "The hand must neither be held so strict as to confine and make the horse uneasy, nor so loose as to not let him feel it. The moment he obeys and answers it, yield the bridle to him; this will take off the stress and relieve his bars, and in confirmation of this maxim, which should never be forgot, which is to caress and reward him for whatever he does well. The moment that the rider perceives that the horse is beginning to place his head, to go lightly in hand and with ease and pleasure to himself; he should do nothing that is disagreeable, but flatter and coax, suffer him to rest awhile, and do all that he can to keep him in this happy temper. This will encourage and prepare him for greater undertakings."

It was nearly 2000 years later before any more books were written on equitation. Early in the sixteenth century many books were written, but they dealt primarily with the high-schooled horse and the one trained in manege. This training is now taught in dressage.

From prehistoric times until the sixteenth century there were no horses in North America. There were fossil remains of Eohippus on nearly all of the North American continent, but for some reason the horse disappeared long before the discovery of America. Somewhere between 9000 and 7000 B.C. something exterminated all the horses on this continent. There were no horses here until 1509, when Cortez brought eleven stallions, five mares, and one foal. With these horses the Spanish riders brought the start of our present-day riding which they had learned from the Moors who had inherited it from the Moslems or Saracens.

The Spanish riding school was developed in the sixteenth century and it was influenced by the Moors. With Spanish riders and Spanish horses Imperial Austria started its *Spanish Riding School*. This school still operates in Vienna and is the last of the great riding schools. Anyone who has ever seen the Lipizzaners perform at this school will never forget the thrill.

Thirty years after Cortez landed in Mexico, Hernando de Soto brought 200 horses to Florida. Some were from Spain and some from the larger islands of the West Indies. He set out in search of gold and spent two years looking in vain. He reached the Mississippi River, where he died. At the Mississippi there were only forty horses left. Of these, all but five were slaughtered for food. These five horses escaped on the west bank of the great river, and from these came the first wild horses of the west.

By 1612 the Spaniards were breeding horses in Florida and these horses spread northward and were crossed with the horses of the colonists. From this cross came our Quarter Horses.

The horses of the colonies came from northwest Europe and were first landed in 1541 at the site of Quebec. During the seventeenth century many horses were brought to the colonies from England, Ireland, France, and Germany. The first English Thoroughbred was brought to Virginia in 1730.

Prior to the Civil War most of the men riding on the ranches in the west and taking care of the cattle were Mexican vaqueros. After the war, many Americans from the southern states moved west and began ranching. They brought some horses with them and this seems to be the first real crossing of the eastern horse with its western neighbor. With this came some crossing of equipment.

At that time Mexican-style equipment as well as the Spanish language prevailed on the ranches. The saddle and bit they used, the forerunner of our modern equipment, was, oddly enough, very similar to those used by the knights of antiquity. This style of equipment was brought to North America by the conquistadores of Spain.

At first, the range horses were ridden with a spade bit. These range riders rode with a comparatively loose rein, unlike the rider from the east coast, who was accustomed to the European style of riding. Much can be said for this loose-reined style of riding. The horse trained to neck-rein can pick his way over rough terrain much better if left to himself. (*See* Figs. 199 through 206.)

The breed of the western horse was gradually improved by being crossed with the Thoroughbred, Standardbred, and Morgan. From this cross came our Quarter Horses. The original western horses were small and these crosses increased their size.

Many ranchers had no use for the spade bit horse who needed at least three years training. The spade bit was gradually replaced by the snaffle, halfbreed, and curb bits. This halfbreed bit had a roller in it (called a cricket) which was made of copper, like the bits in the days of Xenophon. It didn't, however, have the spikes! From this era came the grazer bit so commonly used on the ranches of today, where the

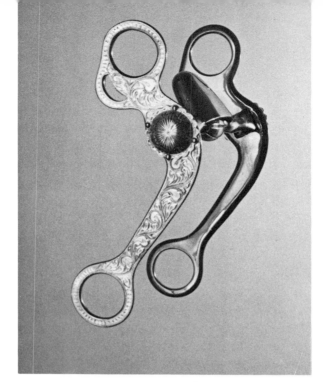

Fig. 199. This is a version of the grazer bit with silver overlay on the sides.

Fig. 200. The Hash Knife.

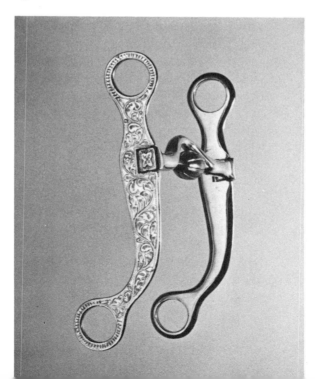

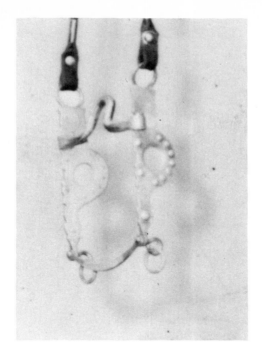

Fig. 201. The open port, Santa Barbara sides.

Fig. 202. Bar or halfbreed mouthpiece.

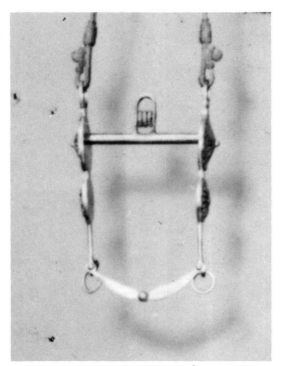

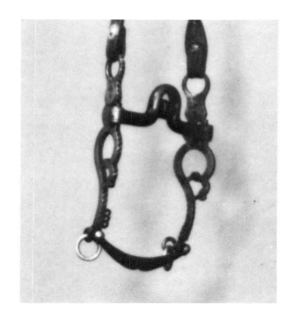

Fig. 203. The port with cricket (roller) in it.

Fig. 204. Halfbreed mouthpiece with "S" sides.

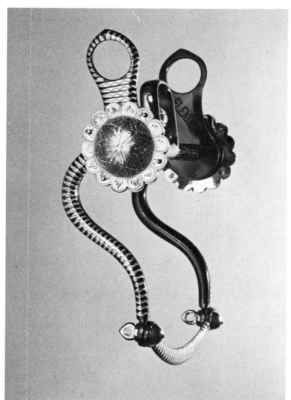

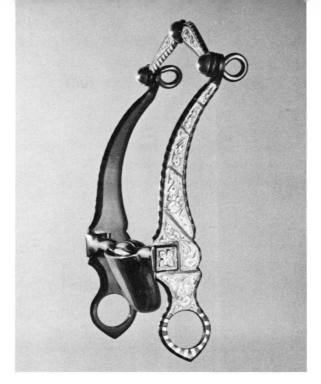

Fig. 205. Port covered with copper shield.

Fig. 206. Spade bit with Santa Barbara sides.

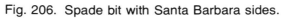

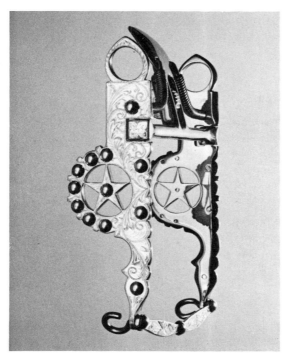

horse needs very little special training after he is "broken" to the saddle.

The Charros of Mexico had preserved the Spanish style of riding and its equipment until the Mexican Revolution of 1911 which ended the Charro rule. California, not affected by the revolution, and somewhat isolated from outside influences, was able to maintain a highly developed form of Spanish horsemanship which is of Arab and Moorish origin.

Many of these Spanish customs still prevail in California where the patient and unhurried ways of the late California Dons produced a supple, controllable horse. Started in the hackamore, gradually put into the bridle, taught the leg cues, and one-finger control of the spade bit, the horse is taught slowly and well. Rawhide reins with the braided romal were used and these customs have spread to the neighboring states of Arizona, Nevada, Oregon, and Washington, where we find the use of this equipment in nearly all horse shows. We find many California ropers using a spade bit and closed reins in horse show and rodeo competition.

This Spanish style of riding has become known as the California style today, while the use of a grazer bit and split rein is now known as the Texas style. I see nothing wrong with these terminologies and again I say this is not an attempt to prove that one is better than the other. (*See* Fig. 207.)

I can say that there is no mechanical means, no contraption, no invention, no method, that can make a horse's mouth responsive and sensitive other than the skill and tact of the rider. There is no shortcut to horse training. The rider must remember that "it is all in the hands."

From this we learn how two distinct systems of equitation have carried through the years. Each has its place and its proponents. The old argument as to the merits of each may never be settled and California-style versus Texas-style will probably always be debated. Only recently has the American Quarter Horse Association approved the use of closed reins and romal. Many Texas and Oklahoma judges penalize the rider for using this equipment even though it is in accord with the rules! Not that many years ago the American Horse Show Association would not recognize a rider with split reins in a horsemanship or medal class, either.

Many horsemen believe that the show horse should have some degree of collection no matter what kind or breed of horse. Herein lies

Fig. 207. Jan Montreuil on Poncho, winning the Youth Reining Class in a competition. This is California-style riding.

a divergence of opinion between California trainers and advocates of Texas-style.

The question of how much, if any, collection is necessary in the western horse depends on what he is required to do. Most trainers believe that the cutting horse or roping horse needs no collection to perform his work or to show. This also applies to the horse ridden on many of the large ranches.

If the horse is to be shown in dressage competition or in high-schooled events he must be fully collected. (*See* Figs. 208 and 209.)

The horse shown in western classes, Texas-style, needs no collection but the one shown California-style does. This isn't complete collection; possibly it should be called semi-collection. (*See* Figs. 210, 211, and 212.)

There are several definitions for collection and, to dispel the idea some hold, collection is not obtained by pulling the horse's head back, causing him to arch his neck. One definition states: "The horse must go forward freely. He must accept the bridle and relax his lower jaw. He must be under control through the reins and by pressure of the rider's legs." Another accepted definition states: "Collection must be obtained by riding the horse forward, towards his head, and not pulling the horse's head back toward his body. Throughout this training it is

Fig. 208. You can start as young as you want—an eight-year-old equestrian riding her horse with full collection.

Fig. 209. Arlene Helm on Truly Bright was the winner of an amazing nine trophies and thirty-two ribbons in ten shows. The horse is fully collected.

Fig. 210. Joan Scallio on Baby Tyler was Maryland's first AQHA Youth Champion. This is an example of semi-collection.

Fig. 211. Gail Lindsey on The Commander was the 1971 All-Around Youth at the All-American Congress, winning the 14-15 Showmanship and Horsemanship competitions. This is a good example of semi-collection.

Fig. 212. Light contact will give semi-collection, the degree needed in western classes.

the object of the rider to obtain lightness in front through increased activity of the quarters."

The difference in riding a horse that is collected and one that is behind the bridle is smoothness. Most loose-reined horses are behind the bridle. They are ridden without steady contact between the rider's hands and the bit. Consequently, rein signals come as a surprise to them and when they come, the head flies up, the nose is extended, and the mouth opens. In a reining class this horse stops with his head high and his front legs stiff. His figure eights are run at speed and his lead changes are often the follow-up type, changing in front and a stride or more later, changing behind. This horse is difficult to show in western riding classes. He either goes too fast, or speeds up when making his changes, and may even miss some of them.

When we speak of reined horses we must mention that great little palomino mare Pokey's Blonde, owned by Melvin Redd of Browns-ville, Texas. She has been showing continuously since 1966 and stood second twice, as national champion reining horse in the AQHA. She is also a champion roping mare and won the Open Reining at Columbus, Ohio in 1967. Figure 213 shows her being ridden by Shorty Russel at

Dallas, Texas. Some think her head too high in this stop but it must be said she was really flying when Shorty said "WHOA."

One of the things the reined horse must do well is stop, "get in the ground," as Texans like to say. Whether split reins or closed reins are best remains unsettled, just as does the question of the right bit for reining. Personally, I believe that the one that works best for you is the one to use! I do believe the closed rein style of riding offers a little more finesse as the rider has the use of his little finger or all his fingers which can produce a little lighter touch than the rider with the split reins uses. (*See* Figs. 214 through 217.) This is true because the rider's fingers are more supple than the wrist!

We must remember that in addition to being able to stop, the reined horse must be able to turn around! He must roll back in the patterns prescribed by the AQHA and this must be done just as he comes to the end of his slide. He must make a half turn and go in the opposite direction.

The horse can roll back under one condition only. His pivot hind foot (the one on the inside of the turn) must be ahead of his other hind. Thus, if he rolls to the left, the near hind must be ahead. When this doesn't happen he must take a step ahead or back before he can turn. (*See* Figs. 218 and 219.)

The routines asked in the Quarter Horse shows are described in detail in the rule book and each judge has the right to choose the one to be used in each class. Some trainers believe that the horse schooled to these patterns is not as good a reined horse as one able to perform unexpected patterns prescribed by the judge at the start of the class.

The AQHA patterns are not popular with exhibitors in the shows on the west coast although they are used in Quarter Horse shows. The largest shows there are called open shows because they are open to all breeds. The rules of the AHSA are generally used and the reining classes are called stock horse classes. They emphasize the long slide and stop as well as many spins and different types of figure eights.

Californians are very critical of the way a horse handles his head when he stops. The horse that throws his head high, opens his mouth, and stiffens his body will get little consideration. (*See* Figs. 220 through 228.)

The closed reins must be held without your fingers between them. The fact that split reins may be held with one finger in between them has occasioned much controversy as to whether this should be allowed. I don't like to hear the word cheating being applied to this way of

Fig. 213. Shorty Russel on Pokey's Blonde makes a flying stop in Dallas, Texas.

Fig. 214. Dwight Stewart on AQHA Champion Thunder's Sally at the AQHA convention in Las Vegas, Nevada. Mr. Stewart rides with a closed rein because it offers him lighter control.

Fig. 215. Imprint Foremost, one of the great reining horses, ridden by owner-rider Mike MacDowell makes a fine stop.

Fig. 216. Short O'Cash ridden by Randy Fowler tied for ninth at Columbus, Ohio, 1975. Mr. Fowler uses a split rein.

219

Fig. 217. Dale Wilkinson rode El Ricky Breeze with a split rein to tie for third in the Futurity. What Figs. 214 through 217 demonstrate best is that you should use what works best for *you*.

Fig. 218. The roll-back. The pivot hind foot must be ahead of the horse's other hind foot; to roll left the near hind must be ahead.

Fig. 219. The roll-back completed.

Fig. 220. A fine stop by Iralena, ridden by Kenny Dunlap, owned by Dwight Stewart. The reins are not too tight and the horse's head is in good position.

Fig. 221. Tom McDowell making a fine stop on Taco Fair Berg.

Fig. 222. This is a poor stop. The horse's head is too high.

Fig. 223. Whoa! A poor stop; the rider has pulled hard enough to lift the horse's head and open its mouth.

Fig. 224. An excellent stop. Note the good position of the horse's head.

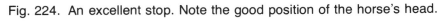

Fig. 225. Ladybird Linda ridden by Barbara Green stops poorly with her head high and her mouth open.

Fig. 226. This is an unusual stop to say the least.

Fig. 227. The rider is high in the saddle and a little heavy handed, but the horse is stopping.

Fig. 228. Denito Dar shown at the All-American by Bob Anthony.

holding the reins. I don't believe that the rider who uses closed reins should be accused of riding with two hands.

Again this is the California system versus the Texas way and either way of handling the reins is permissible in the rules. I believe that anyone who has ridden reining classes or stock horse classes will agree that it is necessary, at times, to lengthen or shorten the reins while performing the difficult patterns of those classes.

So, when we examine the rider with the split reins, we find he must have a finger in between them to make these adjustments, walking his fingers up or down the reins as the condition requires. The accomplished rider can shorten one rein or the other while doing this and can get the effect of the direct rein as well as that of the bearing rein or neck rein. As long as this is in compliance with the rules I don't believe it should be called cheating. Whether this should be allowed is an unsettled question.

Conversely, the rider who uses closed reins can't have any fingers between them and so must be able to adjust the reins by using his other hand. If he does so, and returns his hand to his thigh and maintains the required sixteen inches of slack between hands, I don't believe this is cheating either. (*See* Figs. 229 through 232.)

Many arguments are advanced for each style of riding and the advocate of the California style does not claim that it is easier to ride that way, but rather, that it takes a better trained horse, which is the prime belief behind this riding style.

The desired slide and stop can best be done by the rider timing his stop to that fraction of a second in which the horse vaults over his leading foreleg. At this time the horse's hind feet are off the ground and a squeeze of the rider's legs causes the hind legs of the horse to shoot forward under him. Collection? Yes, I think it is collection because the horse comes down with his hind feet well under him. If the rider elevates the forehand through the reins and if the horse maintains the proper head position, his slide is a thing of beauty. The rider should not try to hold the front end of the horse in the air; let it come down and then, with another light pull, check him again. The horse then slides behind, with his legs locked under him. The front legs either run along or touch the ground several times during the slide. He will stop in a collected position from the pressure of the rider's legs.

The rider who leans far back in his saddle, sticks his feet ahead, and applies hard pressure through the reins will find it nearly impossible to keep the horse's head down. This is called the stiff stop. The muscles in the neck, shoulders, and forelegs are very tense. The slide where the

Fig. 229. Jablee with Chris Watkins up.

Fig. 230. A stiff stop, the horse is "getting in the ground," though his head is too high.

Fig. 231. Jet, shown at the All-American by Charlie Dodds.

Fig. 232. Big Bob Cody, owned by Sharon Reichard and ridden by Mike Allen, won at the 1975 All-American Quarter Horse Congress and was second at the 1975 World Championship Quarter Horse Show.

forefeet touch the ground several times cannot be accomplished by this rider, as the horse's head must come up.

The method of driving the horse's hind legs under him while he is suspended on the leading fore is often called *riding into the stop.* A horse slides and stops better when he is accelerating than he does when he is slowing down! Strength is not the answer to a good stop. (*See* Figs. 233 through 240.)

The secret of making the finished horse lies in the way the reins are handled. The horse learns to work properly by repeating over and over again the same system of handling the reins. They must strike his neck at exactly the same place each time a particular lesson is being taught. The signals to him must come from the same place each time. A signal given too high or too low can cause the horse to become nervous. Good stops are not accomplished by force or accident.

California and many other states have state fairs, county fairs, and district fairs which receive money from the state derived from pari-mutuel handle at the racetracks. In 1971, this amounted to a little more than $360,000 in California which was returned to the fairs for prize money! These fairs conduct yearly horse shows for all breeds. Some of these shows are very large and run for as long as ten days. Two thousand entries is not uncommon. There are many divisions of

Fig. 233. Excellent form by Clene Continental, ridden "into the stop" by Dale Wilkinson.

Fig. 234. Ronnie Sharp's legs aid this horse in a nice stop. Note the good head position and closed mouth.

Fig. 235. Poor position in the saddle by Kim Smith, but the horse is stopping.

Fig. 236. Sugar Bars Dude ridden by Larry Rose placed second in the Futurity with this performance.

Fig. 237. Scotty Ingersoll on Redwood Breeze was the winner of the Junior Stock Horse Class at Santa Barbara, California, in 1974 for doing such a job as this.

Fig. 238. In this stop, Kim Myers and Zipper Cody show form that would be hard to improve upon.

Fig. 239. High Proof—trained and shown by Bob Anthony and owned by Willow Brook Farms—was the 1974 World Champion Junior Reining Horse and the 1975 World Champion "Open" Reining Horse. In 1976, he was named the Champion Senior Reining Horse of the Florida Gold Coast Circuit.

Fig. 240. Tawny Cody—another Bob Anthony/Willow Brook Farms effort—was the 1974 Champion Senior Reining winner at Louisville, Kentucky. She is an AQHA champion.

classes as well as classes for many breeds. To mention a few of these divisions, classes are offered for lightweight and heavyweight (1100 pounds being the division point), open, green, ladies, men, juniors, amateur, owner, costume, stallion, mare, gelding, and championship classes.

The problem in California has become one of keeping the classes from getting too large, so cross-entering isn't allowed! A pleasure can't enter a stock horse class or vice versa and a hunter can't enter a jumper class or vice versa or the classes would be so large the show would never end.

One of the most popular classes on the west coast is the hackamore class which is divided into a hackamore pleasure class (*see* Figs. 241, 242, and 243), and a hackamore reining class (*see* Figs. 244 through 249).

The use of the hackamore (jáqima) is a tradition on the west coast. To enter this class, the horse must never have been shown in a bit other than a snaffle, must not be more than five years old, and ridden only with a braided hackamore. Those who believe in the ways of the California Dons and retain the patient and unhurried ways of these early day horsemen consider the hackamore a basic training method for the future stock horse or reined horse. (*See* Fig. 250.)

Fig. 241. Lynn Stickler is on Samedi Bar, a fine hackamore pleasure horse.

Fig. 242. Mike MacDowell on a fine hackamore pleasure horse. This is a popular class which affords the green horse an opportunity to gain valuable experience.

Fig. 243. Minnie Schoen shown by Lynda Olson made ROM in hackamore pleasure in sixty days.

Fig. 244. Dwight is shown here after winning the hackamore class at Scotsdale, Arizona.

Fig. 245. A fine stop for a hackamore horse made by Hoo Dewdrop, ridden by Gary Long, owned by the BarNone Ranch.

Fig. 246. The "Old Maestro," Clyde Kennedy, winning the hackamore class with the stop he's put on so many horses.

Fig. 247. Gary Baumer on Jacob Break winning the hackamore class at the Cow Palace in San Francisco, California, 1975.

Fig. 248. Linda Baker winning the hackamore class on Astro Chex, the Champion Hackamore Horse of 1971.

Fig. 249. Ronnie Richards, one of the top California trainers, on Burt Brown, the 1971 Pacific Coast Champion.

Fig. 250. A hackamore is made up of a bosal, headstall, and mecáte. This is a beautiful bosal made by Luis Ortega, the greatest in his profession.

Most trainers prefer to ride the green colt in the snaffle bridle for a few days to keep from skinning his jaw. The trainer then places a hackamore under the bridle and rides the young horse with both and then removes the bridle and continues with the hackamore. Occasionally, a young horse will become "heavy" on the hackamore. At that time it is wise to return to the snaffle bridle for a few days. Alternating between the hackamore and the snaffle bridle works well for some. If the colt's head is too high, the running martingale in conjuction with the snaffle bridle is a fine training device, but very few trainers believe that a standing martingale or tie-down should be used with the hackamore or bridle. (*See* Fig. 251.)

Perhaps the most important thing to remember about the hackamore is that it is a two-handed instrument and was never intended to be ridden with just one hand! This is contrary to the beliefs of the American Quarter Horse Association for their rules state that only one hand may be used on the hackamore reins when showing in a class with bridle horses. Can this be because the hackamore horses were beating the bridle horses? (*See* Fig. 252.)

Knowledgeable hackamore trainers use only the bosal (the braided nose band) with the rawhide core, for the cable core causes the bosal to be too severe and it doesn't shape to the horse's nose. The true hackamore man will use nothing but a mecáte (reins and lead rope) made of horsehair. This may be as large as one and one-half inches in diameter at the start. As the colt progresses in his training, smaller mecátes are used until the time he is ridden "straight up," when the mecáte may be as small as one-half inch in diameter. To make the mecáte and have enough left for the lead, the hair rope must be about twenty-two feet long.

The mecáte is slightly prickly to soft hands, but most trainer's hands are not soft. If this is a problem wear gloves. This prickliness of the mecáte is designed to attract the colt's attention to it against his neck and to aid in teaching him to neck-rein.

Successful operation of the hackamore depends on the rider's hands. As he rides with a rein in each hand, he tries to avoid any steady pressure on the bosal. He also tries to avoid a pull with both reins at the same time. The give and take method, or pull and slack, if you prefer, produces the horse with the "good nose." At the same time it teaches both lateral and vertical flexion. The horse's head can be placed high or low depending on what the rider does with his hands. To set the horse's head the rider must remain alert. He must think like the horse all the time he is riding, for the colt is learning all the time the

Fig. 251. Brian Doner on Somebody Bars shows a snaffle and running martingale.

Fig. 252. The hackamore is meant to be ridden with a rein in each hand.

rider is on him. The rider must anticipate a young horse's actions and be ready to turn him in a small circle and keep his head up before he gets out of control. If it's too late, it's too bad!

During this phase of hackamore training the colt is taught the flying change of leads which he must use in reining and stock horse classes. If his basic training was done well he has learned to take either lead readily; the left lead in response to pressure of the rider's right leg and the right lead in response to pressure from the rider's left leg.

The flying change of leads, or, if you prefer, the "change in the air," has always been difficult to teach to anyone other than an accomplished rider. In this the horse and rider must work together and their timing must be exact or the correct change can't be accomplished. The horse's preliminary training must have been done properly. It now becomes apparent why it is imperative to teach the horse to take the right lead on pressure from the left leg and the left lead from the right leg cue.

To effect a correct change is not easy and a fault commonly seen is the horse who changes first in front, and then behind. This is called the follow-up change. Here, the rider has to lean sideways to get the horse to change, and, when he does change in front, it is not until the next stride, or some later stride, that he changes behind. This is poor technique. During the interval before he changes behind he is disunited or cross-leading.

Worse than that are the changes seen in many shows, wherein the horse changes in front and the hind change does not take place at all. There must be no sideways motion of the rider's body at the time of the change.

Again, it must be said that to train or show you must ride well. We find that until the rider can distinguish precisely which lead the horse is loping on and tell by feel he should not try the flying change. If the rider must look down at the front leg, or look at the horse's shoulder to discern the lead, he is not ready.

The accomplished rider can tell which lead the horse is on by feel. This is the way it must be for there is no time for any other method of determining which lead is involved. As we learned in Chapter 9 the lead can be felt by the rider if he will notice which side of the horse leads, which side is ahead, which of his feet is ahead, and which hip is ahead. This is the feel of which I speak. Remember, in the figure eight you must not change direction until you have changed leads!

Speed is not the answer to the flying change of leads. Almost any horse will change if he is going fast enough. The well-trained horse is the one who will change on cue, while going at a slow lope or canter. The sequence of foot falls at the lope and the canter is the same.

Although we learned the sequence of the footfalls at the lope in Chapter 7, I think a review will help to better understand them.

Let's agree on terminology before we start. The correct terms are: off hind for right hind; near hind for left hind; off fore for right fore; near fore for left fore. The near side is the left side; the off side the right.

There is a moment of suspension between each stride of the lope, that fleeting moment in which the horse floats through the air with all four feet off the ground.

Say we have a horse loping on the left lead and so the first foot to strike the ground after suspension must be the off hind, followed by the near hind and off fore together, and lastly the near fore, and again into suspension. There can never be any doubt about the lead when we understand that if the off hind strikes the ground first he is on the left lead: always the opposite lead from the first foot down.

The first foot down is also the first foot to leave the ground and is often called the *push-off foot* or *trailing hind*. As we will see in the pictures there is a time just before suspension in which the horse is supported on the leading fore, in this case the off fore, and he vaults over it, much like a pole vaulter does with his pole. (*See* Fig. 258.) This is referred to as the time he vaults over the leading foreleg. This leg helps him to go into suspension. This is the critical time in which he is cued by the rider for either the flying change of leads or the slide.

The flying change of leads must be made by the horse during that fleeting moment in which he floats through the air.

In Figs. 253 through 269 we see the left lead going into suspension, but he must come down on the right lead. If the rider can control the hind legs, the forelegs will take care of themselves. Seldom do we see a horse on the correct lead behind and wrong in front.

The horse that went into suspension on the left lead must put his near hind down first, followed by his off hind and near fore together, and lastly the off fore (the new leading fore). Then he vaults over the new leading fore and goes into suspension again.

It is best to remember that it is not easy to make *one* correct change of leads, and to make a number at close intervals is extremely difficult!

Explaining the timing of the change is not easy. The rider must transmit his message to the horse in time for him to change while in suspension. If the message arrives too late, the horse must go through the whole sequence of foot falls and change on the next moment of

Fig. 253. Suspension on a left lead. Suspension is the beginning of the sequence of footfalls.

Fig. 254. The first foot down after suspension is the off (right) hind.

Fig. 255. Next down are the near (leading) hind and the off (diagonal) fore, landing together.

Fig. 256. The next foot down is the near (leading) fore.

Fig. 257. The "push-off" hind leaves the ground, rocking the horse onto the near (leading) fore.

Fig. 258. The horse vaults over the leading fore and into suspension.

Fig. 259. Suspension on the left lead.

Fig. 260. Suspension on the left lead.

Fig. 261. At this point the horse must change leads, both front and rear, while in the air.

Fig. 262. The near fore must pass the off fore and come down first.

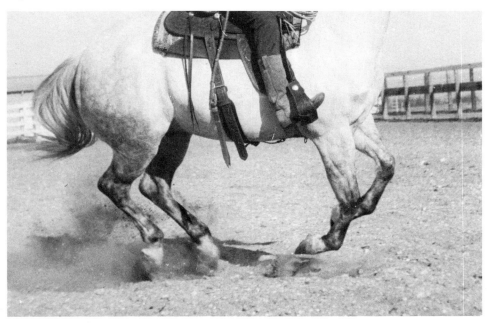

Fig. 263. Still in suspension, the near hind has passed the off hind and the near fore has passed the off fore.

Fig. 264. The left hind is coming down first.

Fig. 265. The near hind on the ground, the horse is now on a right lead.

Fig. 266. Off hind and near (diagonal) fore striking together.

Fig. 267. The off (now leading) fore touches down.

Fig. 268. The horse vaults over the new leading fore having made a flying change of leads.

Fig. 269. Suspension on a right lead. The horse can change again at this point, though most trainers recommend waiting at least four strides.

suspension. From this we learn that the time to send the message is at the exact instant he vaults over the leading foreleg and by the time the message reaches the horse's brain he is in suspension and makes the change.

I am often asked whether a horse can change leads on every stride. Some horses can, but not all. In dressage competition they may be required to do this, but the horse must be driven into the bridle to the point that it takes a strong hand on the reins. Obviously this won't do for the western horse who must be ridden with a reasonably loose rein, or with light contact. The western horse should not be asked to change more than every fourth stride.

In teaching the young horse to change leads it seems best for the rider to step up in the stirrups and place his weight a little farther forward just as the horse vaults over the leading fore. This helps the green horse but is not necessary with the finished horse.

When the trainer believes the colt or green horse is ready for the flying change he will work him a little while in the Dressage Figure Eight, trotting the cross overs and loping the circles. Then he will lope to the center of the X and (assuming the colt is on the right lead) squeeze with his right leg as the colt vaults and change him to the left lead. The colt will speed up a little at this squeeze and, though a little acceleration is not harmful, he should not be allowed to increase his speed very much. Later in his training he should not be allowed to accelerate at all.

If the colt changes as asked he should be brought to the walk and rewarded by both voice and a pat or two. The green horse will sometimes miss the change behind and if this happens he should be brought to the trot and started again on the correct lead. Do not hit him with the bat or frighten him. Nothing should be done to frighten or to cause him to lose his confidence.

As we have learned from the study of horse psychology the horse quickly picks up a routine and seems to delight in beating the rider to the maneuver. This is especially so in the change of leads at the figure eight which is used in so many stock horse and reined horse classes. Consequently, when the horse has perfected his change of leads he should not be ridden in the figure eight very often or he will develop the bad habit of changing before the rider cues him.

To avoid the horse's speeding up from leg pressure at the change many trainers put the change in the reins. This method uses a slight lift of the hand, just as the horse vaults over his leading fore to cue him to change leads. This way there is no acceleration and it doesn't cause him to switch his tail or kick out as some horses do from too much leg pressure.

Many trainers believe there are only a limited number of fine stops and lead changes in a horse and that when these are used up, the horse begins to decrease in efficiency.

The AQHA lists the Western Riding Class under working classes. This is not only a popular class, but it is also an excellent test of horsemanship. It requires a series of lead changes in addition to the other requirements of the class. It is a good class and we find many pleasure horses and a few reined horses being shown in this class. (See Fig. 270.) In this class, the horse is asked to proceed quietly through a gate, over a log, lope a zig-zag course, come to the center of the pattern, stop, and back readily.

Many exhibitors believe that the faster a horse goes in the figure eight the better the score he will receive. This is not so! Nearly all horses will change when going at speed, but the trained horse is the one who will change at the slow lope or canter. Speed in the figure eight in the stock horse class will get you the "big thumb." Out!

The footing in many arenas is not good for the long slide. A good

Fig. 270. John Ness winning the Western Riding Class on Rock Hornet.

slide can only be done on tanbark or some surface that is solid underneath, with a loose, thin layer over the hard surface. There is no way a horse can slide in sand.

Sometimes the arena has been watered too much and is slippery. This is the time when the well-trained horse, who can make the flying change at a slow speed, gains an advantage. A horse going rapidly on such a surface begins to slip and may even fall.

The rules in nearly all western classes specify that the horse must be backed. Of course, he should back readily and straight, with his head in a normal position and his mouth closed. This is especially true in a stock horse class, and we often hear the expression, "he runs backward." He may appear to run backward but he really trots backward for his diagonal legs move together as they do in the trot. A well-trained horse can back rapidly, though not in deep sand or mud. (*See* Figs. 271, 272, and 273.)

Much has been said about how to teach a horse to back in a previous chapter. To sum it all up, backing is riding backward with continuous leg pressure accompanied by light rein pressure. The horse will back until both pressures are released. Training the horse to back is not

Fig. 271. Backing is an unnatural motion for the horse. The near fore and off hind move together here. The horse moves the diagonal legs together when backing as in the trot.

done by force. A capable trainer can teach his horse to back as rapidly as he wishes.

There is one more maneuver the reined horse must master—he must turn around. These turns are known by various names such as pivots, quarter-turns, half-turns, off-sets, hinges, and spins. None of these are difficult to teach if the horse can be collected. He must have his hind legs well under him to execute these turns, and to do them with speed as required in the show ring. It is unnecessary for the rider to spur the horse in the shoulder or bat him on the side of the head as we have seen some inexperienced trainers do!

Remember that the horse can turn under one condition only. His inside hind foot in the turn (the pivot foot) must be ahead of the other hind foot.

Collection is necessary because the horse needs his hindquarters well under him so that the fore hand becomes lighter. He turns with most of his weight on his hind legs while his forelegs push him around.

To get the horse to make these turns, the rider's hand is raised slightly and the horse is reined in the direction of the turn. The rider leans a little back and in the direction of the turn and exerts pressure

Fig. 272. In backing, the rider squeezes with the legs to create impulsion.

Fig. 273. Resist forward motion with the reins while maintaining leg pressure until the horse steps backward.

255

with the calf of his leg that is on the outside of the turn (left leg for right turn). Actually, the rider uses both legs to keep the horse collected and the hindquarters under control but the outside leg creates the impulsion for the turn.

The horse should make at least a quarter-turn before his forefeet return to the ground and push him up and around again. Each time the forefeet strike the ground the rider repeats the squeeze of his leg or the use of the spur to speed the turn. Some trainers prefer using a bat or training whip to the spur. If either of these is used it should be applied just behind the outside leg of the rider. A series of pivots become the spin and impulsion speeds it up.

Collection becomes more important as the horse advances in his training. As we think of collection we must realize that it is the act of riding the horse forward toward his head and *not* pulling the horse's head back toward his body. We are attempting to obtain lightness in the front of the horse through increased activity of the quarters. To get this increased activity, the rider must create added impulsion by active pressure of his legs or the use of the spur. If we accept this as a definition of collection then to back a horse into the turns, pivots, or spins can't be right!

As a horse spins he must keep the pivot foot nearly in place while the other hind walks around it and the forefeet push him sideways each time they return to the ground. His hind feet should remain in a circle no larger than two feet in diameter while his forefeet lope around it. If he is turning to the left he is in reality loping on the left lead.

Some inexperienced trainers, usually in a big hurry to produce a reining horse quicker than the old trainer down the road, attempt to teach these turns by batting the horse on the side of his head. They get the horse to turn, but in an incorrect manner. The horse turns both ends around as though suspended in the middle. This is called the merry-go-round turn. This turn can never produce the desired pivot, spin, or roll-back of the finished horse, nor can the trainer expect his horse to be relaxed, supple, and confident.

Teaching these turns is not difficult if basic training was thoroughly done; if not, it must be completed before the horse can advance to reined horse status. Circles are, again, the trainer's life-saver. Without them to school the horse on, his mount would soon pick up the routine and anticipate at every opportunity. The preliminary training for the turns is best done while riding in circles at the trot, not the jog. The more extended the trot the easier it will be to roll him back over his hocks. As the green horse is trotting in the circle he has no way of telling when you are going to ask for the turn and so he doesn't "prop" or hesitate, expecting the turn.

Both the bearing rein and the direct rein are needed for this, so it is best to ride with a rein in each hand. The direct rein starts the colt's head in the new direction and the bearing rein assists. While the colt is trotting briskly the rider squeezes with both legs to collect the colt and turns him to the inside of the circle at the time his inside hind foot is ahead. Just one step or movement of the turn is asked, then he is returned to the trot again. The colt should not be stopped at this time or all impulsion will be lost and he must be restarted. The rider should not turn the colt until he stops of his own accord but should settle for an eighth- or quarter-turn before proceeding at the trot.

The trainer can encourage the colt with his voice and there is often time to give him a pat on the neck to let him know he is learning his new lesson. Patience is the answer rather than the bat on the side of his head or the spur in the shoulder.

It has been said that a horse can't turn around until he has stopped and this is true in a sense. However, he can be brought to a halt in which his feet have stopped moving ahead but he still has momentum and impulsion of his body. This is exactly what we want to happen at these turns on the quarters. Some trainers explained this as "he stops but he doesn't." If the rider can maintain the impulsion in the colt's body he is still mobile and can turn with ease. If he is brought to a complete stop he can't turn and must be started again.

These turns can be overdone in training. The young horse soon tires of this and should not be compelled to make more than a few turns without being relaxed and walked around the ring once or twice, after which the lesson can be resumed. In all the turns, pivots, and spins don't stop him, ride somewhere, anywhere, but don't stop! For instance, in the spin, if you turn until he stops of his own accord he will begin to stop sooner each time you spin him. Before long, he won't spin at all. If you spin and stop at the end of it the same thing begins to occur. At the end of the spin go somewhere—it doesn't matter where. (See Fig. 274.)

In 1667, Newcastle's second book, *A New Method To Dress Horses*, states: "The understanding of a horse is infinitely degraded below that of man by several who notwithstanding, by their actions show that they believe the horse to be the more intelligent of the two. And indeed, a boy is a long time before he knows his alphabet, longer before he has learned to spell, and several years before he can read distinctly; and yet there are some people who, as soon as they have got upon a

Fig. 274. The spin is one of the last maneuvers the horse learns. The horse is reined in the direction of the turn as the rider leans back a little and exerts pressure with the leg on the outside of the turn.

young horse, entirely undressed or untaught, fancy that, by beating and spurring, they will make him a dressed horse in one morning only."

In gathering and arranging the material for this book I have been guided by the fact that basic training must be the same for every western horse. Fortunately, there are many practices common to both western and English riding. I have tried to illustrate the fact that you must teach only one thing at a time. I want trainers and trainers-to-be to realize that there are no shortcuts to horse training. After the basic training is completed the western horse has only four things to master. He must become proficient in the slide and stop, the flying change of leads, backing, the roll-backs, and spins.

There is progress! As recently as 1970 exhibitors and trainers in the midwest differed from the west coast in their way of riding, their attire, appointments, and the equipment they used. This year at the first big shows (Fort Worth, San Antonio, and Houston) very few riders used the fringed saddle blanket which I always thought presented a bad appearance. Now we see many beautiful saddles that are clean and polished, with nice stamping and some silver. Seldom do we see a rough-out in a show class nowadays. More beautiful silver-mounted headstalls are being shown, although too many are still using the old aluminum grazer bit.

In Chapters 8 and 9 I have tried to show pictures of riders attired in many ways, so that the impact of a nice costume could be compared to plain working clothes. I firmly believe that appearance attracts the judge's eye and affects his decision. This is what the show's about; the exhibitor is trying to catch the judge's eye and make him watch his performance.

I do not believe that a suit jacket is proper in a western class except in showing in halter or showmanship classes. Loose-fitting clothing of any kind detracts from your appearance. This is *show* business and anything that makes the rider and his horse more attractive helps toward winning!

In conclusion I want to say, be proud of your horse and his condition, be pleased with your attire and the appointments of the horse. Ride proud! Be tall in the saddle!

Recommended Reading List

Blake, Neil French, *The World of Dressage*. Fort Collins, Colorado: Caballus Publishers, 1973.

Campbell, Judith, *The World of the Horse*. New York: Thomas Y. Crowell Co., 1975.

Chamberlin, Brig. Gen. Harry D., *Training Hunters, Jumpers, and Hacks*. New York: Arco Publishing Company, Inc., 1972.

Chenevix-French, Charles, *A History of Horsemanship*. New York: Doubleday, 1970.

Connel, Ed, *The Hackamore Reinsman*. Cisco, Texas: Longhorn Press, n.d.

Denhardt, Robert Moorman, *Quarter Horses: A History of Two Centuries*. Norman, Oklahoma: University of Oklahoma Press, 1967.

DeRomaszkan, Gregor, *Fundamentals of Riding*. New York: Doubleday, n.d.

Edwards, E. Hartley, *The Horseman's Guide*. Levittown, New York: Transatlantic Arts, Inc., 1970.

Ensminger, M.E., Ph.D., *Horses and Horsemanship*. Danville, Illinois: Interstate, 1969.

Felton, W. Sidney, *Masters of Equitation*. New York: British Book Centre, 1972.

Fillis, James, *Breaking and Riding*. Fort Collins, Colorado: Caballus Publishers, 1973.

Glyn, Richard, ed., *The World's Finest Horses and Ponies*. New York: Doubleday, 1971.

Hatch, Erich, *What Goes on in Horses' Heads*. New York: G. P. Putnam's Sons, 1970.

Lea, Thomas, *The Hands of Cantú*. Waltham, Massachusetts: Little, Brown & Co., 1964.

Littauer, Vladimir, *Commonsense Horsemanship*, 2nd ed., New York: Arco Publishing Company, Inc., 1972.

——————————, *Schooling Your Horse*, New York: Arco Publishing Company, Inc., 1956.

Seunig, Waldemar, *Horsemanship*, rev. ed., trans. by Leonard Mins, New York: Doubleday, 1961.

Simpson, George G., *Horses: The Story of the Horse Family in the Modern World and through Sixty Million Years of History.* New York: Oxford University Press, Inc., 1951.

Smythe, R. H., *The Mind of the Horse*, 2nd rev. ed. New York: British Book Centre, 1973.

Trippet, Frank, *The First Horsemen.* New York: Time-Life Books, 1974.

Tuke, Diana R., *Bit by Bit.* New York: Arco Publishing Company, Inc., 1965.

Vernam, Glenn R., *Man on Horseback: The Story of the Mounted Man from the Scythians to the American Cowboy.* Lincoln, Nebraska: University of Nebraska Press, 1972.

Williamson, Charles O., D.V.M., *Breaking and Training the Stock Horse*, rev. ed. Hamilton, Montana: Williamson School of Horsemanship, 1968.

Wynmalen, Henry, *Dressage.* New York: Arco Publishing Company, Inc., 1971.

Xenophon, *The Art of Horsemanship*, trans. by Morris H. Morgan. New York: British Book Centre, 1972.

Young, John Richard, *Schooling of the Western Horse*, rev. ed. Norman, Oklahoma: University of Oklahoma Press, n.d.

Zeuner, R. E., *A History of Domesticated Animals*, New York: Harper & Row, 1964.

Index

About the Author

For five decades Dwight Stewart has bred, trained, and shown fine horses. At the age of five, his father set him astride an old gray mare and started a love affair that has lasted into the present.

When Dwight turned sixteen, his family moved to California. Here he learned the unhurried training methods of the Spanish dons from such well-known trainers as M. R. Valdez and Bill Goodwin. These methods of schooling the young horse to hackamore, bit, saddle, and leg resulted in a supple, responsive mount much to young Stewart's liking. This schooling is integral to the Stewart style of teaching horse and rider.

As a young trainer Dwight Stewart had to take the wilder, more cantankerous horses. He has been kicked, bitten, bucked off, rolled on, and run away with. Despite all this, Stewart has survived and prospered.

Today, twenty-four Quarter Horse Champions and countless horsemen give Dwight Stewart credit for their successes. The great Quarter Horse Stallion Major Thunder—a Champion of Champions—is one of these. First trained, now owned by Dwight, Major Thunder's record fills four pages of the Quarter Horse Record.

Stewart has established and operated successful training stables in California, Nevada, and Arizona. Today, he operates from his ranch in Texas. He is past president of both the California Cutting Horse Association and the Arizona Professional Horsemen's Association. He holds both AHSA and AQHA judge cards.